# Knowing the Score

# Knowing the Score

## Play-by-Play Directions for Women on the Job

### BETTY LEHAN HARRAGAN

ST. MARTIN'S PRESS, NEW YORK

Stiles for
Relaxation
(503) 281-6789

Design by Laura Hammond

Library of Congress Cataloging in Publication Data

Harragan, Betty Lehan.
  Knowing the score.

  Includes index.
  1. Women—Employment.  I. Title.
HD6053.H28  1983     650.1'024042     83-9794
ISBN 0-312-45870-3

First Edition
10 9 8 7 6 5 4 3 2 1

*This, too, is for my daughter Kathleen
and for her cohort of future high achievers:
The Class of '84*

# Contents

# . . . Behind This Book

All the people in this book are real. The episodes they describe, the problems that haunt them, the doubts they disclose, the anger that floods them, are contemporaneous with the 1980s. You could be one of them, although only you will know because the identity of contributors is well disguised. Even so, you might recognize a boss, a co-worker, a subordinate, a relative, a friend, a secretary or a casual acquaintance you met at a networking conference.

You will recognize these individuals, of course, only if you are one of today's 43-plus million working women who considers herself genuinely ambitious and is determined to avoid as many pitfalls as possible in your struggle to climb the proverbial ladder of success. It doesn't matter what occupation, field or profession you're in, nor does it matter what level you've reached. My informants cover the gamut of jobs currently held by a cross-section of achievement-oriented women, yet the stories they relate about daily incidents at work bear striking resemblances to each other, despite the drastically different functions.

How I came to be the receptacle for confidential outpourings by thousands of career women around the country explains the origins of this volume. Back in 1977 and 1978 when the early editions of my first book, *Games Mother Never Taught You*, were printed, the publicists were dismayed to find that their time-tested outlets for promotion—book reviews, magazine excerpts, national television shows—proved curiously insistent that "their audiences" wouldn't be receptive to encouraging women to aim high enough in business to compete successfully with men—on men's terms.

The lone exception to this petrified mode of thinking was MS., which can hardly be described as a "business" publication. Its female editors knew that women readers would be intensely interested in anything that helped improve their grasp of the economic realities involved with making a living. They were right, as subsequent developments proved. Nowadays, I am sought out and interviewed by magazine, newspaper, radio and television reporters, many assigned by the same media that only recently thought their readers uninterested in business subjects. At the end of November 1982, *Games Mother Never Taught You* was fictionalized and dramatized as a CBS network television film starring Loretta Swit as a beleagured, ambitious working woman. Five years ago, such an eventuality was considered a joke; today, the dual-career marriage has become a staple of the 1980s.

To get back to the origins, I was the only one not surprised by the turn of events years ago; indeed, I had cautioned that it might be so. But I was thoroughly unprepared for what happened to me privately—I began to receive letters and phone calls from total strangers who were bubbling over with eagerness to tell me their job problems. Maybe male publishers and producers weren't interested in gamesmanship for women at that time, but their female employees certainly were! Clerical assistants sneaked off with advance copies their bosses disdained, while information-hungry women purchased the book or borrowed it from the library. I could almost track the distribution pattern from postmarks on unsolicited fan letters.

In general, women readers thanked me for explaining the mysteries that bedeviled them at work, then went on to describe the circumstances they found themselves in and requested amplification on what they could do to improve their lot. A surprising number located me by telephone to ask if I'd talk to them or address a group of women with whom they were associated. This kind of response astounded me (my experience in this field was nil) because I had no idea that readers wrote to authors. I still don't know if that's a common occurrence but to this day I regularly get passionate letters and impromptu phone calls from heretofore unknown new readers. As always, they tell me about puzzling or traumatic developments on their job and want advice for their personal situation.

That's how it started, but that was by no means the end. I began to accept the speaking invitations and during the ensuing years I have traveled to all but a handful of the fifty states and the provinces of Canada, in many cases returning several times to the same or different cities in a state. Each of these trips brings me into close contact with hundreds of local women, in almost every conceivable white-collar occupation, all over the country. We spend time together enjoying long discussions, exchange opinions about the status of women's career options in that region—and invariably there are the intimate confessions of personal job dilemmas. I collect so many business cards I'll never straighten them out unless I buy a computer because the mobility of modern American women is a phenomenon not yet appreciated by employers or the travel industry. Luckily, many of the women I meet keep in touch over the years and let me rejoice in their progress or sympathize with their disappointments.

In view of my mounting job-problem collection, it was inevitable that I should want to disseminate this wealth of information to other women seeking answers along the same lines. So when Judith Daniels and Susan Edmiston, then the top editorial executives at *Savvy*, asked me to write for their new magazine, I knew exactly what kind of column women wanted: One that addressed the specifics of a detailed job situation, analyzed the various components, explained what was going on, and recommended strategies or actions to best cope with the problem. Even the smartest of women, who have a sound grasp of the working environment, can lose their perspective when they face an emotionally draining confrontation at work. Those equally smart, but lacking sufficient experience and concrete information, needed to gain the detachment necessary to perceive the games of business in process on the everyday practice fields.

My column, based on this reader question-and-answer format, appeared uninterruptedly in *Savvy* from April 1980 through November 1982. Since December 1982 it appears monthly in *Working Woman*. This book is an extenuation of my running dialogues with self-identified ambitious women. It includes the three-year collection of articles that appeared in the magazines, but it is much more than that. These columns generated an independent flow of communications—by mail, phone or in person. As I traipsed around the country I got enormously positive feedback from women. Some said they loved to discuss the subjects with friends over lunch each month; others admitted they often photocopied a column and passed it along to a friend or associate (occasionally, an adversary) who was making the very mistakes described. I also discovered a cadre of executive male readers who did exactly the same thing—in hopes, they said, that a female subordinate or associate (or lover) would "catch on" and realize why her present behavior was counterproductive within her job setting. If some of my recommendations in the following pages sound overly dogmatic, you can be sure that the inflexibility of that unwritten business rule has been substantiated by a significant number of experienced women (and men) who concur.

Not all of the reaction was blithely approving. Sometimes a topic I thought was obvious and benign sparked surprising controversy. Not infrequently, outraged purveyors of fallacious information I attacked in a column came back at me with a vengeful pen. Loads of women contributed variations on a theme and offered further insights. In several instances I was deeply grateful to individuals who caught me up in an error of fact or statement. Some of them have allowed me to use their real names when reproducing their eloquent comments. The point is, I learn constantly from the members of my lively communications network, and I think others can benefit as much. That's why a great deal of the disputatious reaction is synthesized or quoted under the relevant topics. In addition, quite a few women's questions are answered here for the first time.

So much for the background of this book. How to best utilize the information contained herein requires a bit of explaining. Unlike a carefully plotted text, this one does not pretend to cover the standard range of women's possible job problems. Its contents were dictated by those asking the questions, which automatically steers it toward the province of information *gaps*—those bits and pieces of factual knowledge that are too often glossed over or reported without a context. The chapter groupings have an internal logic from a superficial point of view, but if the truth be told many of the questions could as easily fit in a different chapter. Real-life job problems do not come in neatly labeled boxes that can be lined up in alphabetical order like spices on a shelf. Rather, each is a convoluted construction with countless tentacles that are apt to pop out and engulf anybody or anything in the vicinity.

The index is your most trustworthy guide through the maze. There, you can locate any subject that concerns you and follow its trail down a dozen winding paths that weave in and out of several chapters. If nothing else, that exercise should convince you that we working women are all connected in subtle and mysterious ways. No one is alone in a hierarchy.

Lastly, I want to extend my heartfelt greetings to all of you whose anonymous voices resound strikingly throughout this volume. You have a common bond that you're unaware of. You have all told me you feel isolated and alone, cast adrift on a desert island in the labor force, with no one to talk to, no one to trust. Not any longer. Here are lots of other women with whom you can strike up endless, fascinating, imaginary conversations—or stimulating arguments. The wonderful thing about them is that they all speak your language.

# CHAPTER ONE

# Increase Your Odds
# in the Working Game

The point of this book is to make you happier in your ongoing role as a working woman. Since this book is composed almost entirely of job problems, that may sound like a contradiction. But consider the implications. Happiness is a state of optimism and satisfaction. It contains a generous ration of faith that luck, prosperity and good fortune will come your way. On a more comprehensive level, it suggests that one is well-adapted, comfortable, effective, open to adventures and undismayed by challenges.

By that definition none of us is consistently happy about our job situation. As gratified as most American women are (or should be) that the ideal of equal employment opportunity has been introduced to our culture, the reality of coping with everyday complexities on the job is often beyond our comprehension or preparation. Somewhere along the line many of us got the impression that working outside the home would be a life of wine and roses. Nobody warned us (could anyone have foreseen?) that the wine might be sour and the roses badly withered. In fact, few of us seriously examined these female expectations: Who was supposed to deliver the vintage wines and dewy nosegays of success and prosperity to our outstretched hands? Heaven knows that solons of industry have been trumpeting warnings about overoptimism from the very beginning.

At the start of women's massive influx into the permanent workforce—a mere five or ten years ago, remember—the requirements looked easy enough to meet. Go to college or vocational school and get

1

the proper training for your chosen profession. Then get a job, secure in the knowledge that employers are mandated to select candidates from the best qualified, academically superior, regardless of color, creed or sex. From then on it would be automatic: Promotions would be accorded to those who worked hardest, produced the best, took on added responsibilities and demonstrated their value to the company. If such devotion was not rewarded with a managerial job, you could take your case to the personnel department, which would be eager to place you in a position commensurate with your talents because, of course, the company's main concern was retaining such valuable employees as yourself.

It shouldn't have taken long for that chimera to disappear into the bog it came from, but unfortunately it did not. Countless women, to this day, are putting their career fate into a basket of excess academic degrees and their faith in an intangible commodity called "hard work." In subsequent chapters you will notice the frequent reiteration of phrases such as, "I knocked my brains out," "I worked evenings, weekends and lunch hours," "I broke my neck to do a good job." An extraterrestrial might conclude that human females have an ineradicable tendency toward masochism—but an earthbound pragmatist can see that working women are operating in the job world from a base of illusion instead of a grounding in facts. If there were any truth in the myth of "hard work," many women would have zoomed to the top executive ranks in the past decade because few employees work harder than ambitious women. But the reverse has happened: Hardly any women have kept pace with male colleagues of the same age and very few can be said to have zoomed.

Clearly there is something missing from the formula that "Hard Work equals Success." It is the same ingredient that I set out to isolate nearly ten years ago, a search which culminated five years later in my book, *Games Mother Never Taught You*. At that time I labeled the missing x-factor as "perspective" or the realization that working is a *game*. And I confidently predicted that if women incorporated this essential factor into their career calculations they could outwit the entrenched white male hierarchy. I still believe that. Furthermore, I've had hundreds of ecstatic reports from a wide cross-section of women that substantiate my conviction. Over and over I've been told how the concepts of gamesmanship have helped these women break through career barriers, refocus their aims, avoid drastic mistakes, gain deserved promotions, and, most satisfying to me, negotiate substantial salaries and raises.

None of these desirable results are achieved by women who do sloppy work or are careless performers—most of them admittedly work very hard—but they have learned to evaluate the component of "hard work" as merely one element in a complex formula for getting ahead in the male-dominated working milieu. Put in gamesmanship terms, they have grasped the principle that rewards are earned on the strength of how well one plays in the game, how well one reacts to the challenges when *out on the playing field*. That is a far cry from passive reliance on "hard work." Viewed in perspective, hard work is a basic requirement for getting into the game in the first place; it is tantamount to the athlete's physical training, warming-up exercises, practice sessions and drills. Technical proficiency does not set you apart, *it makes you one of the crowd!* At best, it indicates to scouts and coaches that you are potential material. But the only quality that makes you stand out from the crowd is the way you handle yourself when given a chance to get into the real game of working.

Predictably enough (if they don't know they're playing a game), a great many women fail at this juncture. You can see the evidence all over the labor landscape as previously advancing women are "plateaued," "leveled off," transferred to dead-end positions, or terminated under one guise or another. Not all of these hapless occurrences can be traced to failures of the individual, of course. Many current career interruptions are attributable to staff cutbacks mandated by the poor economic climate, to continual realignments within corporations, to turnover of chief executives, to foreign competition, to cuts in funding, to a host of factors beyond the employee's control. These are called "the breaks in the game," "the luck of the draw" or some other euphemism for acknowledging that luck plays a part in everyone's game.

In a sense, gamesmanship can be viewed as a way to maximize your odds in a game of skill and chance. As undesirable as a recession is, bad business times do not negate the need for gamesmanship; they intensify it. That's because better players are those most apt to survive cutbacks, and because adherence to the rules is more strictly enforced. The margin for error is narrowed considerably—and that puts women at a great disadvantage. Women are, after all, comparative rookies in the games of business. They have been out on the playing field for only a few short years, and much of their experience is still limited to farm teams. As the overall economic games become tougher and more competitive, fewer men are willing to take a chance on neophytes so we see a mounting backlash of discrimination against women and nonwhites. At the same time, less competent white males are being ousted from the game, so even though discrimination is thriving, knowledge of gamesmanship can help counteract it.

During the past several years women's appreciation of gamesmanship in business has increased by quantum leaps. Had the American economy stayed on track I suspect that women would have maintained their upward progression dating from the mid-1970s. But women were barely launched on lifetime careers when the economic confusion of the 1980s descended. Aside from practical difficulties (unemployment, paucity of jobs), the turbulence within institutions has served to muddle women's tenuous hold on the operative rules. With their growing awareness of political games as vital ingredients for upward mobility, many women are putting so much emphasis on "playing internal power politics" that they forget this is an old-fashioned serious *game* to experienced men and that it operates on mutually agreed rules, regardless of economic conditions.

What I see happening to many women who think they "know all about the game" is equivalent to a wild scramble; they blow as the wind blows, impulsively responding to moves by co-workers or stubbornly defending a preconceived notion. This is game-playing at a primitive level. It's as if they are playing checkers and looking only to their next immediate move, while business games are akin to chess where skilled players mentally plot several moves ahead before they touch a pawn. Obviously, such calculation takes a lot of practice as well as a thorough grounding in the rules of chess: knowledge of the board, the relationship of the variegated pieces, the directional moves allotted to each, the options open to opponents, the time span involved. An extra advantage is knowing your opponent's style of play so you can more accurately predict the moves you might expect in retaliation. (A trenchant argument for staying with one employer rather than chasing rainbows in search of the "ideal" company.) Even in the stress of a crucial moment there is no latitude for a chess player to ignore the underlying rules—especially not with a rank amateur's complaint: "But I don't see *why* the pawn can't move sideways when a rook can."

Chess illustrates the complexity of business games from the vantage of the multiple, nonidentical pieces and their intricate relationships, but it is not a true analogy because chess pieces have no volition; they are pushed around by a master player. However, if you could animate a chess board and turn each piece into a human being responsible for making its own appropriate move at the right time and within the strict rules laid down by the master, you'd have a situation roughly comparable to that on the average job. Indeed, once you make that imaginary transference you've got another game. Football, for instance. Or baseball, hockey, volleyball, basketball—any group sport. Essentially these are games where people are the playing pieces and all those under the direction of one master (or manager) are closely related because they belong to the same side. You'll notice that this group identity doesn't make all the human playing pieces alike, nor invest them with identical properties; it merely lumps them together as an integral unit where the moves of one impinge on all the others.

In modern business jargon, any assemblage of disparate players under the aegis of one superior is increasingly known as a "team." That sports connection has been an accepted image in large organizations for most of the twentieth century, but its relevance was known chiefly to men inasmuch as women were excluded from the teams until the 1970s. Historical familiarity with working teams is one reason men are almost unconsciously attuned to the game's rules and the interlocking relationships, while women are in the position of consciously memorizing canons that are new to them. Not surprisingly, men who are inexperienced, have had poor tutors or an atypical upbringing are finding it very helpful now that women have forced this heretofore unstructured learning out in the open. Some men are even charging "reverse discrimination" on the grounds that they weren't given formal indoctrination into the business world. Consequently, many companies have decided that women don't deserve special attention. "Ready or not," they seem to be saying, "get out on the field and fail or succeed by your own wits."

Contrary to many female impressions, gamesmanship is neither optional nor an extraneous dimension of anyone's job. The game mentality does more than pervade the working environment—*it is part and parcel of functioning acceptably as a paid employee.* The more skilled you become at playing the game well, the better your chances for moving ahead, expanding your horizons, gaining respect from colleagues, and building your own confidence. By the same token, the more fouls you commit, the more flubs you make, the more co-workers you irritate, the less likely you are to feel satisfied with your job and be happy with your lot. Even if you aren't wildly ambitious (or if your grandiose plans got sidetracked), the benefits of learning to play the working game well are incalculable.

Without question, the most obvious indicator of inadequate game skills is a pervasive dissatisfaction, or apprehension about your job. That's not to say each day should be an idyllic experience, but a job should be more fulfilling than aggravating, more engrossing than bewildering, more absorbing than frustrating, and more hopeful than discouraging. If the balance is all on the wrong side of the ledger, you are sorely misplaced in your occupational niche or you are not able to handle the normal run of conflicts and demands that are indigenous to every job. If you aren't comfortable coping with the everyday exigencies of working, chances are extremely high that you don't fully understand the rules of this game.

Other indicators of gaming deficiency are: (1) the occurrence of a totally unexpected event (getting fired when you thought you were safely ensconced); (2) not anticipating a usual result from action or inaction (not getting a raise because you never asked for one); (3) repetitive difficulty with someone or some issue that upsets your peace of mind ("I'd love this job except for #.&.*..!"); (4) confusion about what to say or what to do when action on your part is unavoidable (doing nothing is possibly the worst gamesmanship of all).

No matter what the provocation, most women sense when they are "having a problem on my job." It's easy to say, "Well, everybody has problems at work, that's to be expected." True, but women today have specific kinds of problems and will continue to have them as long as the stereotype persists that women are suited for only a few types of work. Those women who accept these outmoded, traditional definitions of their ability—and don't rock any boats by trying to break out of restrictive slots—don't have significant job problems beyond universal irritations. Such women may hold fancy titles, but if they insist they "never had any problems" you can be pretty sure they are in an "acceptable" function for women and pose no threat to any man or management.

For most ambitious women, however, "problems" are endemic to any and every job. When a problem arises, action is called for, but the kind of action one takes depends on a host of factors contained in the immediate situation—just as a chess move or sports response depends on what else is happening around you at that particular moment. Some women (mainly young, inexperienced ones) ask for a list of guaranteed One-Two-Three Rules that apply to all situations. That's a tip-off that they are looking at their job as a classroom test assignment, rather than an action game. (Did you ever hear of a college coach evaluating freshmen varsity candidates by giving them a pencil-and-paper test?) It's important not to confuse the idea of "rules." There are definite rules you must understand fully in order to assess your moves and calculate the probabilities of winning your point, but there are no immutable directives on how to maneuver within the constraints of these regulations. Gamesmanship, like proficiency in sports or cards or chess, is a *process*, a developmental skill that requires constant assessment and reassessment of on-the-job conditions that are in constant flux. For example, at any given moment, a basketball player can elect to shoot for the basket, pass the ball to a teammate, or dribble to get himself in a better position. Which option is best (all are within the rules) is a matter of judgment. And that judgment is affected by his situation on the court, the placement of other players (his team and the opposition), the time clock, and his technical proficiency to satisfactorily complete the chosen action. Among the actions he cannot consider are: just standing there clutching the ball; picking up the ball and running around the court with it; knocking down another player who's in the way. If he tried any such illegal actions he'd either forfeit the ball or incur a penalty. Responding to problems on the job is a judgmental parallel: No intelligent maneuver is possible without paying attention to *all the other players on your field of play at that moment!* The rules of the game don't change in the midst of play, but the interchanges among personnel keep the business game in continual flux.

Without question, the impact of other people is the reality of the working game that most women tend to dismiss. As you read the stories in this book notice how often women describe their job situation as if they are the only actor in the drama. Or see how many make career plans without the slightest consideration of who else is already in the occupation, or how many plan to enter. The game concept infiltrates all aspects of working: from choosing a college major, to determining an equitable salary, to fending off sexual harassment, to asking for a promotion. None of the action takes place in a vacuum. Working is not a childish game of solitaire; it is a man's game of rough-and-tumble competitive team sports.

Lots of women reject this comparison; they insist on sitting in a corner dealing their own cards on a private game table. ("I just want to be left alone to do my work without getting involved in stupid game-playing.") That's not okay thinking anymore. I once thought it possible for some women who consciously chose "not to play the game" to survive in a limited job arena for considerable time. I no longer view that as likely. The recession and the projections of a slow-growth economy for the next decade or more have eliminated the conditions that tolerated professed nonplayers. In boom times there is a demand for workers that outruns the demand for trained applicants. Under those circumstances managers are forced to assemble working teams from whatever candidates are available to them. "Bodies" are often needed to fill vacant slots, despite their reluctant attitude toward playing in the game. (Naturally such people will be assigned the most inconsequential posts.) But when the reverse is true—when there is an oversupply of educated, experienced candidates vying for choice positions—managers will select those who have a healthy appreciation of team play, not loners who despise the game.

Reduced to its essentials, gamesmanship is a formalized system of interrelating harmoniously with *specified* other people. This description is light years away from the innocuous platitude that you should "get along with everybody," since getting along with the wrong people can result in technical fouls. Working game relationships are functionally structured. There is a designated way to interact with various co-workers, just as there are permissable and prohibited interactions among ball players on the field. Some of these mandated approaches and prohibitions strike women as cruelly impersonal so they tend to discount such precepts. ("I'm not going to give up lunching with my friends just because I got promoted.") Rejecting the idea that business relationships are expected to be more stoical than social, such women rationalize that they are "more humane." But it's not necessarily true. For instance, "impersonal" can indicate impartiality and fairness, whereas "personal" can conceal strong emotional prejudices. Who's to say which is preferable for an ideal working system?

So far the weight of custom in a male-designed system lands squarely on the impersonal approach, but always within the boundaries of the game rules. You cannot trust to spontaneous instincts or private definitions of ambiguous concepts when operating in the business milieu. For instance, "helping others" is a favored female antithesis to allegedly ruthless impersonality, but it rarely emerges as an unalloyed virtue in action. Few male bosses will be overjoyed to hear from a female subordinate, "The reason I'm late with my proposal is because Mary asked me to help her when her assistant quit two weeks ago." Conversely, the same boss will be equally inflamed if he orders the same woman to help Mary in the emergency and gets the response, "That's not my job, I already have an assignment." Many an inept female gamester blames conflict-of-values when the real culprit is ignorance of the game rules, in this case, flouting the authority principles. Whether you personally agree with the game rules is largely irrelevant; when you decide to live in a foreign country you are obliged to conform with unfamiliar customs if you don't want to be ostracized by the natives.

Clearly, the art of business gamesmanship is a tricky affair. Anything that incorporates so many variables in every decision cannot be learned by memorizing homilies. Prowess is developed by actual practice and everyone has a chance to practice game skills almost every hour of the day. Working games are a process, not a one-shot deal. Successful tactics gradually become automatic and can be used repeatedly throughout your career, albeit with refinements as you become more sophisticated in appreciating the subtleties. No job problem can be solved for all time; new challenges pop up constantly, especially as you move up the ladder with competitive colleagues. Game-playing is incessant, so the sooner you gain command of the rudiments the sooner you'll be invited to spar with superior players, thereby improving your own strategic defenses.

The examples in this book illustrate the kinds of challenges that confront ambitious women every day and explain why some tactics work and others do not. None of the stories in the following chapters are manufactured case histories. Without exception they are real-life incidents from the playing fields of business; they show what is happening to women in the turbulent eighties. They reveal the natural ambivalence of neophytes because, of course, they are one-sided—they describe incidents only from the personal view of the writer. *That is their big advantage as a teaching tool for gamesmanship.* Every woman (or man, for that matter) must make job decisions on the basis of what she can perceive at any given moment from her vantage point.

Romanticists might wish we all had supernatural powers to see inside the heads of everyone around us, know what they think of us and our work, and be privy to secret plans afloat in the executive suites. But we never have that advantage; we have to judge situations from our limited perspective. That's the starting point. Hindsight is also tantalizing, as in "Here's the employee's side of the story; here's the boss's side of the story; who's right?" Who's right is not at issue. Who wins their point, achieves a worthwhile result, makes the least dire mistakes is the primary objective. (You can make a lot of mistakes and still come out on top if your opponent makes worse mistakes.)

Sociologists and therapists might prefer more psychological or background data, but that wouldn't help much. If you're a batter standing at the plate with a 90-mile-an-hour sphere whizzing toward you, it doesn't matter a whit whether you got along with your father, are an eldest child, were valedictorian of your class, or have a mentor. All that counts is that you make a valiant effort to drive the ball away from you by hitting it back, or by getting out of the way if a malevolent pitcher aims a sneaky curve at your head. Sure, the latter is illegal but who's to prove it wasn't accidental? And who benefits if you're out of the game with a fractured skull? In business games it's important to anticipate sneak plays and learn to deflect them. Whatever your background or upbringing, I see substantial proof from women who've done it that anyone can learn to play working games expertly.

The fascination with games so permeates our society that whatever one wants to invest with popular appeal is dubbed "a game." Working definitely does not fall into the category of divertissements. As a game prototype it has a deadly serious antecedent—military strategy and tactics, or "War Games." No matter how far removed civilian organizations seem to be, the military mentality permeates every nook and cranny to a lesser or greater degree. You can see the pattern of military regimentation most clearly in some of the earliest American institutions such as police and fire departments, hospitals, public school systems. These are still quasi-military organizations although their external function is to provide exceedingly humane services. Newer corporate organizations try to blur the inheritance from military units but the similarity comes to the surface rapidly when economic disasters threaten.

The switch from martial arts to the more palatable "game" psychology is comparatively easy because organized team sports encounters have a comparable objective, *to win.* But even when they don't win (which happens a high percentage of the time), business entities, military units and professional sports teams share an identical passion—to survive as an orderly, cohesive force that can regroup or reorganize to get back in the fray as soon as possible. That's one reason the games never end and the rules don't change in good times or bad. To explain it from a different angle, large civilian and military organizations are forced into parallel structuring because the number of participants is unlimited; either can be made up of 25, 2,500, 25,000 or a few million individual members. To avoid absolute chaos, these unwieldy multitudes must be welded into some kind of a cohesive unit and one way to do that is to break up the mob into "teams" of self-contained small groups that are structured into the master unit in an orderly way. The minute you hear the word "orderly," you know there are rules involved and that "orders" have a preeminent place. There is a method behind the madness that often seems to prevail in job situations and understanding the unwritten rules implied in that system is the essence of playing business games successfully.

# BASIC RULES OF THE WORKING GAME

*The Playing Field.* The shape is a triangle (hierarchy) divided by a series of irregularly spaced horizontal lines. The lines are closer together near the broad bottom base but usually tend to be wider-spaced closer to the top. (Most big organizations have a diagram available, which is called an organization chart.) Everybody who works for the same institution is located, at any given moment, on one of these horizontal tiers. (It makes no difference whether the entity is an armed service branch, an industrial corporation, a law firm, a hospital, a college, a government agency, a bank, hotel or department store.) There is no limit to the number of triangles set up within any huge triangle ("pyramid") and the same rules apply even though the individual triangles are weighted differently for scoring purposes.

*The Playing Pieces.* Everybody who works for pay is a participant because they are situated somewhere on the field of play. However, the maneuverability of various players is decidedly unequal, depending on where they land on the organization chart. Women are commonly found in stagnant locations due to systemic discrimination or because they haven't analyzed the game site sufficiently.

*The Objective.* This is a hierarchical game and the goal is to progress from the entry-level tier to the top of the triangle in graduated steps from one level to the next ("going up the ladder"). Since triangles narrow precipitously near the top, most players cannot reach the pinnacle, so much activity in the game takes place in the central realm; there, the objective is to switch from small triangles to bigger ones, or, for experienced players, to expand the one you're in, especially if you can't get out of it ("Pyramid building").

*Scoring.* Scores are calculated in dollars and cents and there is a higher monetary value assigned to each successively higher move ("promotion"). Not all triangles are scored alike. Those in lower-paid fields of employment find the winning score has less monetary value than a different field of endeavor, but the scoring points always count on a *relative* basis so points are awarded solely in reference to the maximum possible in a given triangle. There is considerable difference in scoring points between triangle subsets on an identical field (the same company or division) so those who move ahead in higher-rated pyramids (line jobs) can score more heavily than those who progress further in lower-rated pyramids (staff departments). Novice players should take note that "psychic satisfaction" or similarly intangible rewards do not earn scoring points in a game where the tally registers only in money. Inattention to the real scoring system results in a deficiency of power, prestige, respect and authority in the course of the game because those adjuncts are accorded to players who are steadily amassing monetary points.

*Principles of Play.* All players start at the bottom of a pyramid and aim to work their way up to the next tier, then the next, and so forth. To achieve that progression, it's essential that the existing pyramid *have* a series of higher steps and that no immovable person already occupies the space (two players cannot land on the exact same square). The possibility of accumulating points begins when the player enters the game, that is, starts working somewhere. Prior educational degrees or subsequent credit or noncredit courses don't count by themselves although formal education may qualify the player to *start* at the beginning of a more valuable triangle because each "winner" (department head, manager) can establish credentials for entrants. All of the action takes place on the dividing lines between one tier and the next because all players must attempt to move ahead one notch into a vacant position to score a point. In theory this is a simple game, but the specifics are enormously complex, primarily because each player makes an individual decision about how, when and what action to take to stay in a scoring position. If given free rein, players could create a melee that resulted in mass slaughter as all tried to clamber up the ladder at once. So a host of written and unwritten regulations have developed.

### Universal Regulations.

1. *Every player is dependent on one other player and cannot move in any direction without approval from that attached player.* This is the "boss system" in everyday life and, not surprisingly, it creates the most conflict in the game. The player who seeks approval is called the subordinate and if approval is withheld, the subordinate is all but tied down in a static position. Thus, the objective of individuals is to develop the best of relationships with their boss. That seems easy enough if one is a pleasant, sociable person but friendship, as generally understood, is not allowed. The boss, by virtue of placement on a higher tier in the hierarchy, belongs to a different class, or rank, than the subordinate and that rank must be respected. Heterogenous mixing among the many rank classifications is not permitted, so gaining "visibility" to superior-ranked bosses is a much-prized accomplishment in the game, but only as a grounding for future moves! Bypassing an immediate boss is all but impossible without getting caught in a foul.

Although "boss" is the all-inclusive term used to indicate the next highest person in your local triangle, the boss can have one of hundreds of titles: supervisor, manager, district head, regional director, department chief, administrator, assistant vice-president, general counsel, senior executive, chairman of the board, etc. The title makes no difference—it's the authority relationship that determines the freedom of subordinates. Everybody in the working game has a "boss" and all communications between the levels in a hierarchy pass through a chain of bosses. Consequently, these bosses possess increasing amounts of power and control over more and more subordinates the higher they move, but they exercise that control only through the lesser bosses (that's called the "chain of command").

**2.** *Every player has a stipulated position and a designated area for performance.* In theory every player enters the game with a charge to perform certain tasks (known as the "job description"). In practice there is considerable latitude in defining these tasks as assorted players try to improve their own positions and as the boss tries to maneuver in different directions. But however blurry the outlines, the game rules do not award points for activities beyond the operative job description. This rule often clashes with the rights of a boss to assign subordinates to various tasks so astute players must be wary at these junctures. Aside from the boss, however, no other participant in the game can alter a player's positioning, not even the player herself. It is not allowed that a player arbitrarily perform different tasks than those designated. (This rule is consistently violated by eager beginners who try to expand their duties by taking over more or different work to show personal initiative. While such attempts may serve to keep the player busier during the day, they do nothing to change one's position on the playing field—the principal aim of constructive gaming.)

Most subordinates are one of several peers reporting to the same boss and this is the arena where the working game closely resembles team sports. The boss is effectively the team coach and the subordinates are team members, each of whom has a stipulated position. Coaches can switch players to different team positions, if desired. The player who wins a promotion leaves the "home" team and progresses instantly to the new team—one with different teammates and a different immediate boss. (That's why business game-playing remains essentially the same regardless of job level, and why the game is continual; each promotion puts the player on a more experienced team.)

**3.** *Players may form alliances with peers and lower-level players.* In every game where one rule serves to give undue advantage to a certain player there is invariably a countermanding rule that equalizes the contest. In the working game, the boss's authority over subordinates could paralyze all movement unless subordinates had access to allowable methods to challenge the boss's supremacy. That balance is achieved by allowing players to associate freely with peers throughout the organization and to form alliances with them and lower-level employees they can persuade to join them for tactical reasons. (Carried to its ultimate conclusion, this is the sanction that results in unionization of workers and collaboration among different unions.)

Normally, peer alliances are much less structured. Some tend to be transitory, as when a group of subordinates band together to sabotage an unpopular boss. Alliances, as construed in this rule, are not formal pacts. They are deliberate attempts to persuade others to join together with you to achieve some specified goal—get a program approved, resist an arbitrary decision by the boss, support the promotion of a popular co-worker (including yourself), or vice versa. The natural consequence of this rule is that most workplaces are rife with assorted informal cliques of individuals who use their group influence to manipulate changes or (bosses charge) maintain the status quo.

Peers in this context refer to all players located on roughly the same hierarchical tier as you, whether in other departments or operations or your own. Lateral peers are those who are the same number of steps from the bottom (or top) of their departmental pyramid as you are in yours. Titles and grade classifications are often similar across lateral pyramids in the same organization, and peers are generally assigned to work with peers in cross-department ventures or on projects where functions must be dovetailed. Many lateral peer alliances develop as an offshoot of such work projects.

This alliance rule is exceedingly important in the working game because the continual narrowing of the pyramid means that fewer and fewer players can progress to each succeeding tier in the hierarchy; there is a natural elimination process going on. Inasmuch as competition for openings gets keener at higher job levels, alliances of peers and support from lower-level players often spell the difference between a winning and a losing attempt to gain a promotion. Adroit players try never to leave a trail of disgruntled co-workers behind them as they progress because they may need these underlings as allies at some future stage. At best, they don't want to leave a band of enemies in the lower reaches for fear another shrewd gamester may mobilize these malignant spirits into a career-blocking alliance.

Successful gamesmen understand the ramifications of this rule quite well. Women are notoriously negligent in appreciating the many clever stratagems they could devise around this rule. So far, as story after story in this book indicates, women look upon career mobility as a game of solitaire or a one-on-one duel with their boss. Alliances are not the same as friends (many a working woman has discovered to her dismay that her "best friend" was a member of an adversarial alliance.) Business alliances are formed strictly for game-playing purposes to implement some strategy or to accomplish a one-time goal; the membership can vary enormously and the group is often composed of individuals who don't necessarily like each other at all. Women who aren't alert to what's going on can be drawn into alliances that are harmful to their own ambitions.

This is not an attempt to list all the applicable rules of business gamesmanship, just the three key ones. Nobody knows them all. There are so many fine points to the game that the most successful players rack up violations that knock them out of the game at very high levels. In fact, very few players you'll run into are top pros. In many cases, they bluff! Bluffing can be a useful tactic—so long as nobody calls your bluff—but the risks are high. In the final analysis, gamesmanship is a blend of elementary rules, instinct, practice, and motivation. Common sense goes a long way in figuring practical solutions for tricky problems, as long as you remember that this is an action game. You have to study the situation, analyze your options, calculate the risks, and then do what you decided. No one else will do it for you because they are all too busy playing their own game of getting-ahead or surviving intact. The following examples of other women's job problems will teach you much about the intricacies of gamesmanship, but most of all they will demonstrate that you are not alone in your confusion—loads of other women face these same challenges and we can learn much by listening to each other.

# CHAPTER TWO

# Problems With Bosses

## WHY YOUR BOSS IS SO IMPORTANT

Your immediate boss is the most important person in your job life. This holds true from your first days as a probationary neophyte to the last stages of your career climb. Everybody who works for pay has a boss. The only exception are entrepreneurs who found their own companies and become the boss, but even they are subject to superiors—the backers, the bankers, the brokers.

"Boss" is not a job title; it is a universally understood noun that describes a structured relationship: The boss is the person who exercises authority over you in a working situation. Your boss is automatically "superior" to you in the overall structure of the organization and, because of the relative placement of your two positions, your boss can—literally—define your tasks, determine your progress, affect your performance, evaluate your ability, influence your promotion, decide your salary, and color your attitude toward your daily chores. Given that tremendous breadth of control over your present peace of mind and your eventual career destiny, it is little wonder that the boss relationship is highly charged with emotional reactions toward the *person* who is in that position relative to you.

One of the great advantages of treating business as a game is in separating the personal from the political in job relationships. Within the pragmatic atmosphere of working environments, it makes no difference *who* holds the position of your boss (the rung immediately above you on

17

the gameboard ladder) because the position can change hands many times. The key to enhancing the relationship lies in knowing and accepting the authority invested in the boss figure. Absolute deference to the authority invested in your immediate boss is the undeviating Number One Rule of the game. There is no way you can leapfrog, bypass, overrule, ignore, challenge, disobey, or criticize your boss and not get penalized in the game.

Five years ago, that statement was practically incomprehensible to large groups of women; in fact it was not uncommon to run across women who had no idea who their immediate boss was—they independently "selected" an executive to whom they chose to report. Nowadays I rarely find such naiveté (except among some M.B.A. trainees), but there is still a wide gulf between knowing the rule and carrying it out in practice. The seven examples in this chapter illuminate many facets of the difficulties women encounter when they are unclear about the source and range of the boss's authority. When the woman herself is a boss, this confusion is compounded—by not correctly interpreting her boss's authority, she is unable to figure out the parameters of her own responsibility in the given circumstances.

The authority invested in bosses is a direct derivation from the military chain-of-command, a concept that was adopted in toto by industrial efficiency experts more than 100 years ago. Theoretically, the principle embodies a logical division of tasks and responsibilities from the top of a large organization to the bottom. It's such a natural sequence that you can see the pattern evolve every time a small organization starts to grow. Take a one-person business or activity and follow it as it develops. First there's a jack-of-all-trades entrepreneur, who performs all the needed tasks single-handedly. As the business expands, it becomes necessary to hire assistants, who are given some of the boss's tasks to perform—but always under the direction of the owner, who makes sure the deputies complete the tasks according to plans. When activities increase further, the original assistants then hire their own assistants to take over segments of the job—but since they are beholden to the top boss for their performance, they keep a sharp eye on how well their deputies handle the delegated duties. This process continues as long as the company keeps growing, with each one-time assistant subdividing the overload of work and hiring more assistants to complete specified assignments.

As any organization grows and expands it automatically shapes itself into a pyramidal hierarchy with successive layers of bosses—people who were forced to delegate bits and pieces of their job to hired subordinates once the tasks overwhelmed the capacity of one person. Consequently, the work assigned to any subordinate was once (however far back in the dim past) a responsibility of the boss in charge of that function. The boss's authority, then, is almost absolute in judging and assessing the adequacy of the performance of a subordinate, who was, after all, hired to do part of that boss's job.

In long-established organizations this principle is somewhat obscure because individuals are hired directly to perform tasks that have long since been stratified. In large corporations or government agencies the positions have been defined, described and delineated in formal job descriptions that are then weighted according to the significance of the work entailed and allotted a value—that is, a salary range. These are called job evaluation systems and they exist primarily to establish proportionate wage and salary levels for various types of jobs ("women's" jobs are historically rated lower than men's on a gender basis); but the underlying authority distribution is not disturbed—the subordinate position is always rated as a lesser portion of the boss's job.

Whenever a vacancy occurs on one level in a hierarchy (say your boss quits), then the boss to whom that intermediate supervisor reported reassumes the responsibility because the departed individual had been doing a stipulated portion of the superior boss's job. Poor grasp of this principle can be seen whenever someone says, "They put a new boss in charge of my work." Impossible, because "my" work doesn't exist; every job is but a portion of the immediate boss's assigned responsibility. Whenever a new supervisor is inserted between you and your boss, it means that boss has further divided the duties of that office and, ergo, you have a new boss who can, may and does revamp some of the procedures that previously existed. "My" work can take on quite a different emphasis under a new boss.

This division-of-duties process creates the multilayered triangles of each job hierarchy and simultaneously outlines the playing field of the business game. It should be self-evident that power and authority in this structure always flow from the top down, never from the bottom up. Job responsibilities are designated from higher levels to lower levels, never the reverse. Yet listen to the subordinates in the following incidents and notice how often their complaints about their boss flounder on the issue of the boss's legitimate authority. Women at every level (from one who reports to a president to one under the lowest-level supervisor) make the mistake of disregarding their boss's right (if not duty) to give orders, issue directives, assume supervisory control over the departmental function.

The core relationship between the boss's and the subordinate's work also determines performance evaluations. "Doing a good job" is not an accomplishment that can be judged in a vacuum. According to accepted rules, the only "job" one has to do is what the boss wants done! Making a superlative effort to conclude some task the boss considers unimportant or low priority is a sign of poor performance—and equally poor game-playing. Experienced gamesters develop a keep appreciation of their boss's needs and desires. They become attuned to the *downward delegation* of duties and follow the game's authority regulations. If the boss says "don't do" something, they don't; if told to "do" another thing, they make every effort to comply.

The importance of this obedience rule is underscored by the foul penalties: The most severe infraction of the rules is "insubordination" (refusal to follow the boss's directives) and the penalty is dismissal from the game (firing). Thorough understanding of the authority flow is essential to game proficiency because many bosses overstep their authority bounds with unwary subordinates and it's vital to realize when you can resist unauthorized demands. The division-of-labor principle does not mean that each subordinate is an all-round flunky for a boss (unless hired specifically to become a "gofer" or a general Gal Friday).

For example, an executive who is "told" to take the secretarial notes at a meeting instead of participating as a representative of her project, is being manipulated, because that portion of the department's work has been officially assigned to another subordinate, a secretary. This kind of directive is an aberration of the boss's rights and must be counteracted with one tactic or another. Just *how* a good player goes about deflecting unwarranted orders depends on the personality of the boss. So, finally, the *person* who occupies the position of boss becomes a factor in the game. Interplay of personalities comes to the fore largely when defensive mechanisms are called for. You can reach some bosses with humor, others with persuasive argument, others by subtle education, others by memo, others by persistence, others by group pressure (organizing allies), others by action. Whatever the technique used, it must never infringe on the boss's sanctioned authority.

The natural accompaniment of the authority canon mandates that each subordinate understand precisely how much of her boss's authority has been delegated to her. Overdependence on a boss who explicitly or implicitly handed over certain decisions is exceedingly poor game-playing. Once a boss harbors the feeling, "I'm still spending my time on an issue I thought I trusted to a subordinate," that team member is in trouble; the next thought is bound to be, "Why did I hire (or promote) her?" By the same reasoning, an underling who oversteps her boundaries immediately encroaches on her boss's territory or that of a peer player's operation. Admittedly, these boundaries are often delineated by very fine lines, so there is considerable room for judgment calls when deciding how much feedback a boss expects.

The following real-life case histories approach this conflict from the angle of the subordinate trying to make a judgment call on the behavior of her boss. The confusion most of the women evidence stems invariably from their misconception of the authority rules that dominate the boss relationship. The personality of the bosses is of minor importance except insofar as accommodating to the *style* each uses to convey displeasure or to motivate and redirect underlings. The personality of the storyteller is also irrelevant except when fuzzily preconceived notions hinder her ability to see the situation in perspective and prevent her from making an accurate diagnosis of her "problem."

These episodes are self-explanatory. Whatever responses they produced merely elaborated the inherent faulty reasoning and proved nothing beyond the fact that many women don't like to accept the reality of the rank-and-authority caste system that is built into hierarchical structures. Because the boss relationship is so basic to astute game-players, the most instructive way to approach this chapter is to read the questions and decide how you would handle a comparable situation (or would advise another caught in a similar bind). Then read the answers and see if you identified the crucial elements that contributed to the writer's quandary.

# THE INTRUDER

*Dear Betty Harragan:*

*I'm head of production for a small but widely known company in the computer service industry. My staff of twenty-five professionals includes several managers who supervise employees or outside suppliers. I was hired two years ago after a company reorganization, and since then our sales have exceeded industry norms. My immediate boss is the president with whom I have an excellent relationship. He grants me full autonomy in my area and is fair and reasonable when called upon for policy decisions or to adjudicate disagreements between the marketing director and me. I'm sure he's pleased with my work and is not sabotaging me, but he has one disturbing habit that causes endless problems with my staff.*

*Periodically he appears at my monthly staff meeting and criticizes anything he doesn't like. For weeks afterward my supervisors and managers are demoralized because he doesn't understand our operation and has no conception of our conscientious efforts. For example, he once appalled everyone when he brushed aside one manager's apology for a supplier's delay with a brusque, "Fire them and get somebody else if you can't depend on them," not realizing this particular service was scarce and had taken months of patient development. Recently he asked all my managers to write a definition of the corporate objective. Since we have a published goal statement that everyone knows by heart, they assumed he wanted an expanded, or interpretive, version. He blew his stack when he got the memos; what he had expected was a pure copy of the printed corporate statement. After that, I fired a manager who'd been giving me trouble by refusing to follow my directives and whom I knew all along had provoked the boss's intervention. The incident put the whole staff in turmoil, and there's still a residue of hurt feelings or lack of appreciation. Is there any way I can keep him from interfering with and upsetting my staff?*

*Annoyed*

Dear Annoyed:

No. There is no way you can prevent your immediate superior from keeping tabs on the work coming out of your department or from checking on you and your employees to see if they meet his standards. That is, after all, his assigned responsibility, especially since your boss is also the president.

I agree with your evaluation that you are in no trouble as far as your position is concerned. Clearly, you run a successful operation that more than meets management's financial and productivity goals. You seem to have a congenial staff and to feel comfortably confident dealing with your president. Your situation is enviable, undoubtedly a tribute to your managerial skill.

As you describe it, your annoyance stems exclusively from your boss's demoralizing impact on your subordinates. I wonder about that. Can you really be so self-effacing (considering your high position) that you put employees' hurt pride before your own? Might you be projecting some of your anger and humiliation onto subordinates? It's very hard to single out your own feelings from those you ascribe to others, so I'm going to conjecture that these are Siamese twins. It's well known that most managers select key staff members from among those they feel empathy toward, so it wouldn't be unusual for you and your key associates to be kindred spirits, emotionally.

I emphasize this kinship because I'm sure you could see the solution for your management "problem" if it weren't for emotional blinders. You sound dedicated to protecting your subordinates from undeserved criticism, hurt feelings or any painful upset. No question that protecting subordinates is a Grade AAA quality for a successful manager; but there is also such a thing as overprotecting people, thus shielding them from growth experiences. Your example of how "appalled" everyone was when the boss suggested they could always fire an unsatisfactory supplier is a case in point. Granted, there were extenuating circumstances, but management's readiness to fire or replace uncooperative performers should hardly surprise, much less horrify, adult professionals. Are you trying to "protect" subordinate *managers* from exposure to reality? Are you doing them any favor by preventing them from learning how hard-nosed a competitive business must be? Or how their company's top management expects them to function?

You mention that you later fired a subordinate whom you knew all along had provoked the boss's subsequent intervention. A little bird tells me that the earlier mention of firing someone may have appalled you more than it did your subordinates. Apparently you had been tolerating a staff member who was performing under par for a considerable time. Although this person had been giving you trouble and refused to follow your orders, you procrastinated on handling a serious managerial problem because it required that you get rid of someone.

As a result, your department's reputation suffered and your entire staff got tarred with the sticky brush of not following the corporate objectives. Here's where you *should have* protected your innocent staff members by identifying the lone offender. I can see why that was hard to do—because the culprit was you. As senior manager, you let unexamined feelings or fears obstruct your business judgment—and the blame fell on everyone.

I can tell that you manage an overwhelmingly female staff, because the issues that concern you are so characteristic of over-protected women: feelings of hurt pride, upset, rejection, conscientiousness, confusion, lack of appreciation for "hard work." Your staff appears to be a supersensitive group who takes everything personally and is easily demolished by corrective criticism. Notice how they all goofed up on the corporate-goals assignment. You were no better because you should have alerted them that this was an obvious "test" and should have warned them that stated corporate objectives are not subject to "personal" revision by lower-level employees.

I don't think you should be encouraging this kind of naiveté. You should be holding meetings to teach your staff the facts of business instead of perfecting their individual crafts. As a group, they are too task oriented, and that's why they don't understand what the president is saying when he checks up on your operations. Far from keeping him away from your staff, you ought to welcome his personal appearances. He sounds like a sophisticated executive who delegates authority and gives his managers full rein and fair support to accomplish their assignments. Even when something posed a threat to his responsibilities (i.e., ensuring that the corporate goals are implemented), he didn't descend in a fury and personally take charge of correcting it; he merely asked all managers for a copy of the corporate goal statement, thereby, I presume, hoping to stimulate some concrete thinking. It worked, too; you finally made the decision to fire the obstructor.

He steered. He didn't assess blame or usurp anyone's delegated authority. That is *good* management, not interference. You worry about his upsetting your staff's delicate feelings. It seems to me he preserves feelings that count the most: control, command, trust, self-confidence. You could probably polish your managerial style by emulating some of his techniques instead of catering to immature sensibilities within subordinate ranks.


# THE UNDERMINER

*Dear Betty Harragan:*

*My authority is being so deeply undermined that I can't do my job. My boss took eight months to fill my position—personnel director—because he wanted someone with experience in both administration and career development. He is pressuring me to institute a training program, but I have been so overwhelmed this past year just straightening out the company's sloppy personnel systems that I can't get to it. This week he said the department "lacked professionalism" after an incomplete proposal was sent upstairs while he was out of town. I defended myself, explaining I knew nothing about it. He seemed to believe me—but I'm scared. Today one of my subordinates got angry about her performance evaluation and appealed it to him. This has happened before, and he always gives in, saying he follows a "humanistic" philosophy. Last month he appointed a supervisor for day-to-day operations, and she doesn't give me the respect due a boss. I've always encountered unbelievable hostility and resentment from other people here. Should I tell him to stop undermining me? Who's to blame for this mess?*

*Scared*

Dear Scared:

You have good reason to fear that your job is in jeopardy but you're asking the wrong questions. Apportioning blame never cures anything; besides, there's plenty to go around.

It is always a possibility that a boss is undermining your authority. But if so, the details you sketch don't show how he's gaining anything except a demoralized department. It is more fruitful to analyze what you may have contributed to this mess, especially since you have adopted a job approach that is common among women—frantic, haphazard overworking.

You are bound to be exceptionally well qualified in the requisite personnel skills or you wouldn't have survived the careful search. Apparently your boss was determined to expand the department's services with training and development because he waited to find the right person: you. But once on the payroll, you seemed to forget what you were hired to do. Instead, you poked around and found dozens of things wrong with the existing systems, which you proceeded to revise to your exacting standards.

This reorganization was evidently desirable since your boss didn't interfere. Indeed, when your concentration on revamping the technical "systems" threatened the work flow, he appointed someone else to take charge of day-to-day operations. Maybe he sought to help you by unloading nitty-gritty details to free you for heavier responsibilities.

You sound surprised that you encountered resentment from the staff you inherited. If you'd thought about it beforehand, you would have *known* that you'd be walking into a hotbed of hostility. For one thing, your mere presence instantly demoted all your subordinates. While the position was vacant they reported directly to the VP and had an open line to the top. You were inserted between him and them, blocking that access, so they naturally resented the situation (not you personally). In addition, there are probably a few people who think they deserved the job you got, and their cliques agree. Any of them would be ready to sabotage you, given an opportunity. (The one who released the unauthorized report sounds suspiciously like such a candidate.) Furthermore, existing staff members may feel superior to you because they've been there longer, know the company and its quirks.

From day one you were the outsider. Your first priority was to psyche out the human dynamics, try to win over the staff or at least keep an eye on potential troublemakers. Unfortunately, in your zeal to make a success of the job, you plunged into paperwork and inanimate systems and upset normal routines, oblivious to the impact this had on the suspicious staff. Predictably enough, many flew to their old friend, the top boss, with complaints, and he regularly calmed them down.

The anxiety you suddenly feel may stem from a subtle change in his attitude. He has adequate evidence by now to judge your performance and potential. Perhaps he's in trouble with his superiors because the promised training program is nowhere in sight; possibly the unapproved report caused damaging or embarrassing repercussions. Your fatal mistake was disclaiming responsibility for that incident; as his chief deputy you were expected to be in charge during his absence, whereas you admitted you didn't even know what was going on.

As I see it, you'd better move fast to salvage your position. Ask your boss for a long, private, uninterrupted appointment to thrash the whole thing out. Admit your mistakes where relevant but primarily seek his cooperation as you mend your fences. The lines of authority must be clearly understood by all. This could take the form of circulating a departmental organization chart so all employees know who reports to whom. Also, it will force you to look at the people under you and over you, to understand your duties within this hierarchy. You cannot learn to become a responsive, sensitive, humanistic supervisor without a firm foundation in the chain-of-command structure.

You need practice in taking on responsibilities that are rightfully yours. Try to persuade your boss not to settle complaints himself but to discuss them with you and funnel the ultimate decision from him to you and let you channel the ultimate decision back to the employee (especially if you have to backtrack on a decision you originally made). Then delegate, postpone or scrap any unfinished systems revisions and get cracking on the training program.

# THE ABUSER

*Dear Betty Harragan:*

*I am head of direct-mail operations for a nationwide company and my difficulty is with my manager, vice-president of marketing. Every Monday he calls a staff meeting of his eight group managers and by the end of it, I am psychologically destroyed. He has a very abrasive, abusive manner, and the staff meetings consist of rapid-fire questions directed at each of us, followed by mean, nasty comments if we don't know the answers. The entire department was set up two years ago; most of the others always know the answers because they've been with him since the beginning but I've been here only six months. He seems to have a knack for asking me the one minor detail I can't recall (even if I do, my mind freezes because of the humiliating atmosphere). When I try to explain why a particular figure isn't available or say I'll check the return rate on a certain mailing and get back to him, he blows up and screams, "You've been here six months and still don't know what's going on? Why did I hire you?" I'm in charge of enormous mailings handled through several supplier firms as well as in-house test programs. It's impossible for me to give him projections on results that are still incomplete or subject to variable interpretations. Yet he won't listen to reason. One very nice man he treated this way got himself transferred to another division, and my peers merely say, "You'll get used to it; that's the way he is. He hates people who say, I don't know." He's highly regarded upstairs because our department's bottom line is terrific. Don't they care if he makes us all miserable in the process? I can't stand it much longer.*

*Mortified*

Dear Mortified:

I fear you are suffering the kind of delusion about everyday workplace demands that many women experience once they move into a beginning-level management position. You expect the working environment to be a congenial, social, friendly place where nobody's feelings are hurt. Because of these misconceptions, you are an easy victim of aggressive senior managers.

I don't intend to condone tactless managers who publicly abuse subordinates (there are certainly more sophisticated techniques practiced by equally effective executives), but, as your peers point out, "that's the way he is." You express amazement that upper management doesn't intervene somehow to temper his intemperate style. But think about it: How would his superiors know he mistreats his staff? Except for your charge, there is no evidence. Apparently the turnover of employees is exceedingly low and his department produces great results as far as management is concerned. Either he's a genius at pulling the wool over his superiors' eyes or his methods succeed in motivating his staff to high performance.

There's an old expression: "If you can't stand the heat, get out of the kitchen." Your boss is inclined to operate under that dictum. Presumably he raised no objection when the "very nice" male subordinate who couldn't stand high-pressure tactics sought a transfer, so it looks as though your boss is simply attempting to weed out anyone who can't cope with tough demands. In his own uncouth way, he's testing you—and you don't seem to be meeting the challenge. You are disintegrating.

There's no need to fall apart every Monday morning; you have to change your behavior at the meetings so as not to incur his wrath. Your long-suffering peers have tipped you off, but you aren't following their suggestions. They told you he won't tolerate the answer, "I don't know," yet you persist in deflecting his questions with long explanations or convoluted apologies. Admittedly, you often don't know and you attribute your humiliation to his "knack" for zeroing in on the minor details you didn't expect to be asked. I can't help wondering about this uncanny ability of his.

How come he always asks about "minor" details? Could it be that you are assigning priority or significance to projects under your control that run counter to his idea of priorities? Are you boning up on figures that are already widely known or cluttering your memory with past results when he's only concerned with future directions? If you get so engrossed in the technicalities of your own specialty you will fail to see the broader picture that interests your boss. One solution may be for you to analyze the pattern of questions brought up at these staff meetings and see whether you are going off on a different tangent from your boss, or putting emphasis on results that he has already incorporated into his planning.

On the other hand, when he asks something you don't know, why don't you just *guess* and throw out a number with no apologies? (I'll bet that's exactly what your peers have learned to do.) Since this clear alternative has not occurred to you, I suspect you harbor the conviction that you always have to be right and perfect. Few attitudes paralyze competent women more quickly than the need to be perfect. Probably all your boss wants is a ballpark figure that he can use to make a case with his superiors. The nitty-gritty finalities can come later—and be changed if closer analysis proves it necessary. I can almost hear some of his reports to management: "Early returns on that special mailing looked positive, but later responses revealed unanticipated rejection of specific items in the proposal. We've uncovered important public attitudes as a result of this experience."

You said that your responsibility includes testing new approaches to marketing, so your boss is interested in what you're learning, not in justifying every exploratory process down to the last fraction. It appears that he wants your opinion, your conclusions, your perceptions (albeit in numbers), whereas you hesitate to trust your own instincts as an expert. It's by no means impossible to make projections from incomplete information; that's how all management decisions are made. If every executive decision awaited total, complete, unassailable data, nothing would ever get done.

Your awesome dependence on factual data leads straight to another quagmire that traps overly cautious women. You credit your peers with superior knowledge because they've been there so much longer than you. It's as if you privately feel you deserve more compassionate treatment because your are too "new" or "young" to be fully accountable for your operation. Although your letter contains no doubts about your competence in your field, you nevertheless feel that six months is too short a time to know all the answers. True: Six months, six years, even sixteen years is never long enough to know everything. But it's adequate for an experienced professional to get a handle on the job.

If you stop thinking of yourself as a neophyte in this group and accept the reality that you are the only available authority on your

facet of the department's work, your boss may let up on his humiliating tactics. Maybe he's trying to goad you into proper respect for
your own capabilities.


# THE PROCRASTINATOR

*Dear Betty Harragan:*

*I'm getting an ulcer from putting up with an impossible boss. I've
looked for another job, but comparable openings mean relocating,
which I'm not free to do. I've been associate director of a state
agency department for three years. My boss, the director, is sixty
years old, came up through the ranks and has no professional training in the field, although his subordinates all have bachelor's or
graduate degrees. He got the job title when this department was one
man (plus a secretary), but it has since grown to thirty professionals
and is still severely shorthanded. His boss knows he is incapable of
handling a growth department, so there is a reorganization plan
under way, but that is subject to a personnel department analysis
and subsequent approval by another agency. When I go to my boss
with a business problem, he either tells me to spend nights and the
weekend writing a report, or spouts a series of directives that I am to
relay to my managers or to other departments. Then, after it's done
or in process, he denies he ordered any such thing. Other times he
says he'll get back to me with an answer, but never does. I can't get
the resources, office space, people or computer facilities to do my job;
my staff is extremely overworked. He won't retire because of personal
financial problems, so I'm stuck with him. What can I do to hang
on?*

*Helpless*


Dear Helpless:

Reading letters like yours almost gives me a headache, because
the anguish and stress are oh-so-familiar. Difficulties with incompetent bosses certainly rank near the top in women executives' job
problems. In your case, the predicament is exacerbated by the bu-

reaucratic rigidity; I gather your boss has accumulated enough seniority, tenure, civil service points or political connections to keep
him ensconced until the mandatory retirement age, regardless of
merit or performance.

When a situation becomes as seemingly hopeless as yours, the
logical solution is to get out—find another job—which you've
found untenable. The next possibility is to go over your boss's head
and appeal to his superior. That's no route for you, however, because the senior officer is just as hopelessly stuck with this incompetent as you are. The top executive seems to be taking the only
possible step by submitting a major reorganization plan, presumably to diminish the authority or responsibility of your boss. Unfortunately, as you point out, such a solution requires time and
interminable shuffling through bureaucratic channels before it can
be implemented. Nevertheless, some kind of improvement is in the
making if you can manage to cope for the next several months.

Given all the details you outlined—plus your own relatively high
position in this hierarchy—I can't help wondering why you are
running to this confused, ineffectual soul with so many "business
problems." As a trained professional with considerable experience
in your field (women do not ordinarily become associate directors
without a solid background), you might be expected to make most
of these day-to-day decisions on your own. This is especially true if
your boss is known to upper echelons as one who has been paralyzed by the changing demands of an expanding administrative responsibility. That you and your colleagues have better credentials
and training than your boss is probably no accident; the management (even in a state bureaucracy) may be hoping that you professionals will be able to shore up your boss during his final years.

You didn't mention what kind of a personality your boss is, nor
how you two interact on a one-to-one basis, but there are strong
clues in your letter that you have not grabbed hold of the real
authority *you* have. I sense a streak of dependency that is not appropriate to your administrative title. Why, for instance, should you
let your boss tell you what to tell your subordinate managers? Why
aren't you giving those orders directly or delegating assignments
without his sanction? It appears that you are loath to make decisions essential to accomplishing your task or are afraid to take any
initiative.

Once you know a boss is a procrastinator, you also know he doesn't want to make decisions, either—for whatever reason. In that case, an ambitious executive just goes ahead and does it herself. If the action requires his initialed approval, simply put the piece of paper in front of him and wait while he signs it, simultaneously explaining why the matter is urgent. If a decision does not require his signature, don't ask him about it—handle the request or activity yourself, on your own authority. If you make some mistakes, who cares? Apparently you could hardly do worse than your bumbling boss.

Don't forget: You are a boss, too; your subordinates are dependent on your actions and orders to perform their jobs adequately. Try to perceive yourself from their vantage point. Would they say you were in command of the situation—or just as wishy-washy as your boss? Are you *managing* your area—or are you functioning as a messenger, merely relaying the contradictory directives of your vacillating boss? Also try to envision your achievements from the perspective of senior executives, especially the one who is trying to reorganize the place. Does he see you as a "take charge" person ready for more responsibility—or as a glorified clerk who needs a male boss (however ineffectual) to tell her what to do next?

Many people would seize upon your situation as a golden opportunity to flex their managerial muscles and move into the ready-made power vacuum your boss is creating. They wouldn't be getting ulcers; they'd be relishing the challenge, especially under circumstances where management is ready to welcome all the help it can get to bypass this departmental hindrance.

# THE RESTRICTER

*Dear Betty Harrigan:*

*I work in a nonprofit institution as assistant to a supervisor and am doing fine at the job I was hired for. However, for self-satisfaction and to benefit my career, I've repeatedly tried to take on new responsibilities and become more valuable to the company. My supervisor continually interferes with these efforts, saying they are not part of my job, not what I was hired for. We have no job descriptions because the department head wants to "keep jobs flexible," but my supervisor won't give me any flexibility. He has much freedom but is not allowing me any of it. When I asked, he said it's not possible to delegate more responsibility to me. The department head supported me, saying he realizes I have talents my current job doesn't utilize. Should I complain to the department head about my boss's unfairness in being so restrictive? Maybe he's threatened by my competence? How should I deal with this?*

*Discouraged*

Dear Discouraged:

If there's one characteristic most working women share, it is gullibility. We are apt to believe anything, no matter how illogical, if some vague Voice of Authority intones it. Too rarely do we question the source of our information. You are becoming mired in an untenable job situation because you're operating on the faulty premise that "taking on additional responsibilities" is the way to get ahead.

You can hardly be blamed for believing this popular nonsense because it is spewed forth from many so-called "career development" or "management training" seminars for women all over the country. To quote a few gems verbatim from current brochures in the career development department: "Turn your job into a growth experience by assuming more responsibility." "Make your abilities known to your superiors." "Shoulder a greater share of your boss's responsibilities." "Help your organization achieve greater productivity." "Create your own reward system." And always (what else?) "Become more assertive."

Judging from your letter, you have taken such advice to heart and applied it religiously. But the response from your boss is the opposite of what you'd been led to expect. He flatly told you to "cut it out" and get back to your original job duties. No wonder you're confused and discouraged and blame him for being unfair. But in reality your boss is right and the ill-informed career counselors are wrong. Their advice, far from helping you advance, has set you in conflict with your boss.

Let's examine how this came about. Your job title is "assistant to" your supervisor so, technically, all the tasks assigned to your position were originally delegated from his overall job responsibilities. At some point in the history of the organization it was agreed that certain of that supervisor's duties could be handled by a subordinate; ergo, the job slot you occupy was created. It was not designed for you personally but, like all structured positions everywhere, it is an impersonal compilation of limited tasks and duties.

Then you come along and are hired to fill the position. You decide (of your own volition) that you want to expand or enlarge those assigned duties in the interest of helping yourself and the organization. Some shrewd bosses will let female subordinates get away with absorbing more work because they recognize the benefits to the organization—letting an overzealous woman do twice the work for half the pay. (Just how this frequent result is supposed to benefit the eager-beaver woman is beyond my ken.)

Other bosses, however—and yours is in this category—jealously guard their own area of responsibility and don't like underlings who try to move onto their turf. Since your job is a spinoff from his, every time you take on "more" or "new" responsibilities you are really moving into his arena of operation. He gave you proof that he feels threatened when he refused to delegate more duties to you, telling you it was not possible. What he probably means is that he can't "give away" any more of his responsibilities or there may be none left for him! How does he justify his own position if a subordinate is doing the bulk of his work?

Your confusing situation is further aggravated by the wishy-washy attitude of the department head. You think he "supports" you, but I see no evidence of it. He merely pointed out that you are overqualified for the job you hold. That's not support; that's a danger signal. I sincerely doubt that complaints to him will gain you anything. After all, as the senior executive, he is responsible for the policy that there be no job descriptions. Thus, he ensures that nobody in his department (your boss included!) knows where they're at or when they are performing up to expectations. Indeed, there may be no expectations, just encrusted practices from the past.

This form of subjective, unprofessional management is pretty common in nonprofit organizations. Women in this field were expected to work for the "love of doing good" rather than the normal rewards of money and promotion. It's revealing that you never mentioned salary in connection with taking on new responsibilities. Nonprofit organizations are just as much "businesses" as profit corporations. You must realize this or you will never understand how male bosses and administrative officials think.

Instead of getting discouraged, you ought to actively analyze the institution you work for. Make an organization chart based on who reports to whom; then track the promotion patterns of those who have moved upward over the years. See if any incumbent in your job has progressed and, if so, to where. You may be in a hopelessly dead-end position, and in that case your question is moot because there's no place to go no matter how far you expand your job.

There's a quick test to find out whether I'm wrong about your department head and he is genuinely supportive: Ask him for a promotion that *will* utilize the talents he admits you possess. Otherwise, your best option is to maintain your high level of performance at precisely the tasks you were hired to do. Then try to build a comfortable working relationship with your immediate boss by reassuring him you will stop encroaching on his territory. If you are secretly after his job, first help him get promoted so that his position will be open to you. Or you can ask him to keep an eye out for openings where you could better use your abilities. He may be happy to assist you in order to get rid of you, with your inclination to play every team position except your own.

Whatever the outcome, this experience can prove beneficial to your future development if it teaches you the fundamental verity about organizations (profit or nonprofit) that do have written job descriptions. Namely, that lower-level jobs are defined, described, assigned duties and salary by the management—not by one of the employees who is hired to fill that job slot. Gratuitously taking on more responsibility is a fallacy of the first order because it destroys any possibility of promotion; promotion, after all, means getting a slightly higher job that is described as having "more responsible" tasks and duties than the one below it. Next time, find out exactly what you are expected to do because that—and nothing else—is precisely what you will be doing as long as you stay in that position.

# THE CONFOUNDER

*Dear Betty Harragan:*

*I am an experienced personnel professional in the benefits and compensation area. Within the past year I joined a major financial institution, where I've been assigned to the executive vice president to analyze and write job descriptions for fifty new positions in marketing. Each year this VP gives a department party aboard his yacht and because I've been closely involved with his group, he invited me. I considered this honor an indication that he was very pleased with my work and, naturally, I told my boss, the vice-president of personnel. She said, "I'm glad you were invited," but the next day the executive officer accosted me with, "You told your boss! Why did you do that?" I was shocked but told him, "Because I don't believe in surprising her." It seems that my boss mentioned the invitation to him at a meeting they both attended. Now I'm wondering just how much you are obligated to tell your supervisor—especially if a professional conflict is involved. My boss doesn't have good vibes with the executive VP because he thinks the personnel department is too stodgy and should be more responsive to modern wage and salary patterns. I agree with him so we work well together, but I'm caught between two superiors.*

*Ruffled*

Dear Ruffled:

Don't let this incident divert you from your realistic, sensible policy of keeping your boss informed. You acted properly; it was the male VP who responded impulsively. Once women learn how to function well within business hierarchies (as you have), they are surprised to discover that male executives don't always follow their own rules. Then it's only natural to begin to doubt your own judgment or assumptions about proper behavior under given circumstances.

Probably no one knows better than your male senior executive that it was politic of you to tell your boss about the invitation. If there was any indication in your letter that this man was out to sabotage you, I might conclude that he was using this secrecy ploy to get you in trouble with your boss, since she is bound to find out after the fact and wonder why you never mentioned it. Some men do take advantage of naive women by getting them to undercut their bosses with such admonitions as, "Don't tell your boss about this." However, I see no signs of malice in your situation, so we have to look in different directions to account for the senior executive's strange reaction.

As you know, you are in a staff-service department and your role is to advise or assist other departments within the technical area of your specialty. If there's a fundamental disagreement between these department heads, a staff professional like you can be caught in a bind where loyalty to your real boss may conflict with sympathy for the executive whose problems are your responsibility. This often happens when a strong line manager is at loggerheads with restrictive personnel department mandates and seeks to avoid or modify the regulations. As the staff liaison person, you are charged with maintaining adherence to your department's rules but, by your own admission, your viewpoint has shifted to the line manager's side because you understand his need to upgrade compensation for newly created jobs. Presumably you are (or will be) enlisted to press his case before your boss.

Your professional rapport with the executive VP and his subordinates no doubt accounts for your invitation to join the departmental party; you are viewed as "one of them" rather than a member of the enemy camp. This is surely a high compliment to your performance and personality but it also puts you in a schizophrenic mode—you are, after all, one of the "enemy." By telling your boss (and her telling him), you may have sparked a purely emotional reaction: He treated you "special," yet you reverted to type and showed your allegiance to the personnel department. He could have felt this was a breach of loyalty to his needs because he wants you on his side, not hers. (For all the talk of emotionalism in women, it's clear that men in the work force function on a high level of spontaneous feelings, if not pettishness, in everyday situations.)

There's also the possibility that the relationship between your two superiors is a deep, long-standing estrangement. Years before you appeared on the scene, these two vice-presidents may have been battling over wage and salary policies. You say the vibes between them aren't good but we don't know what really transpired during the conversation about your going to the party. The manner in which your boss brought up the subject could have annoyed him, or she might have insinuated that she merited the invitation instead of you since she's head of the department.

Obviously, these scenarios are pure speculation, but you can never underestimate the emotional content of human relationships on the job when correct behavior on your part backfires unexpectedly. To play office politics successfully, you have to keep alert to relationships between—and among—other participants, not just to your private relationships with separate individuals. In your case, you had no choice; you *had* to mention the invitation to your boss because it involved another department with repercussions on your boss's work. This is a good criterion for deciding what to tell your boss. If you'd simply been invited to a social gathering with a few members of the other department, there'd be no need to report it. You should never treat your boss like a confidante and discuss your private, family or social affairs, but you should relate any information or developments that have a clear business impact.

I wouldn't worry about the executive VP's outburst. On reflection, he will recognize the impropriety of his reaction and might even quietly apologize. In the long run he'll feel heightened respect for you because you treated your boss exactly the way he'd want to be treated by one of his trusted subordinates under similar circumstances.

# THE FRIEND

*Dear Betty Harragan:*

*As marketing manager of a very successful industrial firm for five years, I reported to the president, who was enthusiastic about my ideas and let me install a series of sales plans and advertising programs that gave us a distinct competitive edge. My responsibility*

*was heavy but I loved every minute of it as I watched the company
grow from a $2 million to a $10 million enterprise. I considered
myself one of the management team since I was consulted on everything, and I looked forward to spending the rest of my career here.
Imagine my shock when the president fired me! He acted quite upset
when giving me the weak excuse that now they were so big they
needed an engineer instead of an MBA to direct marketing! I can't
recover from this devastating blow. On top of dedicated performance, I always thought these people were my friends. I got along
well with everybody and often acted as liaison between the president
and sales manager, who fought constantly even though they were
related. The president's wife, who was head of accounting, although
she admitted she cared little for business, always treated me as an
intimate friend and was very supportive when I had a family trag-
edy. In fact everybody confided in me, especially about their problems with each other, which were many. In the past year things were
getting out of hand because the company was growing so fast. Once
I had a blowup with accounting over some letters sent to key customers, and his wife complained to the president that I was insubor-
dinate to her (so he blamed me!). The sales manager often refused to
follow directives and just ignored the president, who was unable to
control him. I finally suggested we call in a management consultant
to advise us. At first, I talked with this consultant a lot, exchanging
opinions and showing him why some of his suggestions wouldn't
work because of the complex personalities involved. I feel he advised
the president to fire me. But why? What did I do wrong?*

*Heartbroken*

Dear Heartbroken:

Professionally you could have done very little that was wrong.
The remarkable growth of the company during your tenure as marketing director attests to your competence and creativity. Not many
executives have such a dramatic record of achievement to their
credit.

But personally you made some poor calculations, and I'm afraid
those are what did you in. The sad part is that your mistakes all
stemmed from decent, humane instincts. You are not the first
idealist to prefer a compatible environment where work can be tem-

pered with "heart," where the feelings of individuals are paramount, where personal relationships evolve from trust as opposed to cold-blooded lines of authority.

Obviously you found a receptive breeding ground for your humanistic impulses in this company. It offered the best of two worlds: an opportunity to display your brilliant marketing skills plus the scope for developing close human ties with associates and bosses. Your sociable yearning was rewarded when other executives confided in you, shared intimate secrets and used you as a go-between to patch up their frequent quarrels.

Under the circumstances, it's not surprising that you came to think of these people first and foremost as friends. You wanted to believe that the world of commerce functions in tune with your reverie—that it is a participative, democratic assemblage of equals. Although your analytic and problem-solving abilities worked supremely well when applied to sales-marketing problems, you discarded these pragmatic techniques once the problem-set included emotions and illusions. Otherwise you could have predicted the mess you were getting into. Because your friendship approach was seemingly successful for so long, you could delude yourself and dismiss the factual reality that these co-workers were first and foremost your employer, your superiors, your peer managers. While you daydreamed, they never forgot your real role. "Friendship," you'll notice, evaporated in a cloud of power dust when you violated the chain of command, when you overstepped the boundaries of superior-subordinate business structure, however informal.

Apparently you handled the dispute about key customers through a face-to-face discussion with your "dear friend" the accounting head. However, she took your vehemence as a challenge to her status and went to top management with a complaint of insubordination from an underling. When the president (properly) supported her, you were stunned. I'd wager you had earlier run-ins of a similar nature that you ignored or excused as personality conflicts. Yet the fact that she was a founder of the firm meant she was a vice-president and major stockholder and would outrank you by far, officially.

Her personal relationship to the president added another layer of complexity: nepotism. This was clearly a family firm and you were undeniably an outsider. Treating business associates as pals or cronies is a dangerous predilection in the most impersonal of organizations, but students of human nature (as well as the police) can tell you it is especially hazardous for an outsider to plunge into an intrafamily fracas. I don't think you would have ignored such red flags if you hadn't been privy to family secrets; your social intimacy clouded your business judgment. So much so that you didn't see what was going on under the surface—nor that you were in a prime position to benefit in a corporation undergoing transition.

The president (with whom you worked so well) must be an extremely able executive to have brought his company so far, so fast. But he is now at a crossroads. His firm has passed the point of continuing as a Mom-and-Pop operation; he is on the verge of becoming Big Business and that requires wrenching decisions. He understands (or the management consultant told him) that he needs sophisticated financial controls, not an amateur merely "keeping the accounts." He's being forced (by growth) to set up a formal hierarchy where rank, status, authority and accountability are strictly defined. He needs experienced professionals in senior management positions, relatives or not.

You were ideally situated to fit into such a slot, but weren't considered. Why not? Because your humanistic attitudes got in the way. You are probably right in sensing that the consultant had something to do with your ouster. In talking to him, you eagerly pointed out where his suggestions wouldn't work because of the "personalities" involved. Such comments alerted him that you were more interested in salving hurt feelings and maintaining the status quo than in the future growth, efficiency and competitive stance of this blossoming corporation. The president already faces enough potential confrontations with his relatives; he needs a clear-headed, objective business ally at his side, not a solicitous friend of the very individuals he may have to sideline or terminate. You became the first casualty under reorganization because you embraced the obsolete system and could be a detriment to effecting the changeover.

If, on the other hand, the president evaded his responsibilities and elected to continue his business as the employer-of-last-resort for all and sundry relatives, you still could not win. Then you'd be up against total nepotism where the prime qualification for promotion and substantial salary is blood or marriage relationship. However deeply you wormed your way into family affections, it's unlikely you could surmount the obstacle that you are not really "one of them." In addition, the business problems are bound to multiply with many executives who don't know how to manage, so the illusive friendliness would disintegrate anyway. Your professional qualifications might even have suffered.

Remember, you have your superb record as a marketing executive to exploit. But in the future, look for a *job* where your business contribution will be appreciated and rewarded. Extended families or communes are usually the polar opposites of effective business enterprises. Humanizing the workplace is a theoretical concept that has a long way to go.

# CHAPTER THREE

# Troubles with
# Co-workers

Psychologists, therapists, social workers and behavioral specialists are having a field day with the widespread problems people have dealing with each other in the workplace. Judging from the many brochures I receive in the mail, there are innumerable seminars devoted to "improving your interpersonal skills." The methods range from identifying the unfulfilled needs of both the other party and yourself, to recognizing the eight to ten "types" of difficult people, to understanding the parent and the child in you and others, to developing your "personal power," to communicating more effectively. The thrust, in general, seems to center on avoiding conflict and perfecting a "win-win" philosophy.

Truly, many people you work with are difficult to get along with. There is much to be said for efforts to smooth the interpersonal relationships in a close-knit group of co-workers. It is especially important to learn how to control emotional responses under pressure because spontaneous venting of anger and tears is not appropriate to the situation in most work sites. That is not to deny the existence or justification of the feelings—it is to say that your behavior toward business associates must be viewed realistically through the lens of that person's significance to you *in the job structure.*

Business is not a social construct; it is a calculated game where the objective is to outwit other players in a structured set-up. There is a limit to tolerance and severe time restrictions. The first order of business is to get the job done and only secondarily to cater to personal idiosyncrasies or weaknesses of performers. Only within that framework can the contributions of psychology be evaluated. Unfortunately, most behavioral therapists have little or no appreciation of the everyday priorities mandated by a hierarchical authority situation so their conclusions—based mainly on the human sensitivities of individuals—can lead women far astray in assessing the proper action required to solve an immediate job problem. (Look back at the chapter on bosses to notice how often this kind of confusion warps the judgment of both managers and subordinates.)

The difficulties with co-workers as demonstrated in this chapter have nothing to do with the psychology of handling people. These stories illustrate the unrelated assortment of issues that crop up relative to co-workers, but are not solvable by psychological methods. In these cases (as many others), the intrusion of psychological precepts could be deleterious to a realistic grasp of what's happening in the circumstances.

# THE OFFICE PEST

*Dear Betty Harragan:*

*One of my co-workers is extremely disruptive. When he isn't busy he drops into my office, or my assistant's, to chitchat or complain. If we ignore his conversational attempts, he flips through a magazine or even reads our mail! If we ask him to leave because we are busy, he comes back later. My assistant and I used to enjoy having lunch at my desk occasionally to catch up on reading or discuss upcoming projects. Invariably, this guy drops in and interrupts, so we're forced to go out just to avoid him and gain some privacy.*

*This man and I are peer-level managers in a corporate staff department of a well-known national company. The situation has gotten so intolerable that I finally complained to our boss about his behavior. The boss acknowledged being aware of it (others on the staff had also complained) and attributed it to personal problems the man was having. He said he was sure the problem would straighten itself out in time. That was six months ago, and if anything, the disruptive behavior has gotten worse or we've become the guy's prime targets. I don't want to go back to the boss because he is either protecting this man or doesn't want to get involved in the problem. Since our boss is director of personnel, there's nowhere else to turn. My assistant and I are getting very angry. Am I wrong in sensing some hostility toward women in this manager's actions—or is he just plain insensitive?*

*Exasperated*

Dear Exasperated:

Coping with difficult or obnoxious co-workers probably causes more job dissatisfaction than the work itself or company policies. In fact, "people problems" are moving to the forefront as an important issue for top-management concern. I don't know why it took men 100 years to become aware of the obvious, because women have always been far ahead in this area—they seldom need to be told that one bad apple can ruin an agreeable or pleasant working group, as your current experience confirms.

Your boss's reaction is typical of men in positions of authority, who often panic when confronted with a personality conflict between subordinates, particularly when the antagonists are a male and a female. Your boss could be protecting a fellow male in the sense of empathizing with family difficulties and thus excusing irrational behavior, but more than likely he is simply running away from the problem by pretending it doesn't exist. In effect he has told you, "Solve it yourself; I'm not getting in the middle."

(By the way, this reaction from your boss should tip you off about the function of the personnel department; it is *not* set up to mediate interpersonal conflicts among employees, an illusion that dies hard with many women both inside and outside that department.)

As for reading hostility toward women in your disruptive colleague's actions, I'd say you're on the wrong track. He seems to be expressing the opposite emotion—that he *likes* you and your assistant so much that he can scarcely stay away from either or both of you for more than short periods. Indeed, he sounds almost obsessed with the urge to be in your presence. That would account for the failure of your repeated attempts to discourage him with polite requests to go away or subtle hints that he's not wanted.

You wonder if he's insensitive. Can there be any doubt? Nothing you say or do seems to get through to him. Like a rubber ball, he bounces right back. It takes a bluntly aggressive approach to make a dent on aggressive or thick-skinned individuals. Have you tried the direct expedient of saying, "John, out!" every time he steps over your office threshold? Or repeatedly using such calm declarative statements as: "You can't come in; I'm busy." "You'll have to leave; we're having lunch." "I can't talk to you; go bother somebody else." By failing to control his constant interference you merely provoke more of the same behavior.

If this pest were a boss or any person with authority or influence over you and your work, you'd have a more complex problem. As it is, you are dealing with an equal; repercussions beyond the personal are minimal. Something in your own attitude or responses must lead him to believe you are his "friend" and can thus be imposed upon. If you and your assistant have become the chief recipients of his unwelcome intrusions, it may indicate that other staff members have taken a strong stand and successfully repelled him. By now, you two are the only ones who continue to "welcome" him outwardly—while seething inwardly.

Perhaps you're one of those women who fear head-on confrontation. In that case you could adopt a different tack. What about putting him to work for you? Exploit his childish clinging by figuring out a list of assignments you could delegate to him each time he drops in to chat. Greet him with enthusiasm, exclaiming about the sudden pressure you're under, and tell him how much you'd appreciate it if he would do you a tremendous favor. Then hand him, for example, a preselected batch of magazines and ask if he'll go through and abstract the articles and information important to you. If he takes this as an invitation to sit in your office while he completes the task, let him. By adroitly using this tactic, you might tie him down in your office so much that the boss eventually gets annoyed and voluntarily initiates the very discussion with him that you wished for.

Could there be another deeper layer of complication here? I sense an intimation that you and your assistant may have established a self-contained outpost in the midst of a large department and you tend to resent any intrusion into your private little bailiwick. Such self-imposed isolation could easily result in magnifying the irritating mannerisms of an innocuous co-worker. Perhaps the ultimate solution is for you and your assistant—independently—to start mingling more with all the rest of your colleagues in the course of the day. Self-confidence in handling face-to-face relationships with a variety of personality types does not come out of magazine columns or books. It's a skill that builds gradually with experience, and there's no better place to practice expert human interaction than in today's office environments.

Evidently the office pest is an ubiquitous phenomenon in the American workplace. At any rate, my advice to "Exasperated" brought a torrent of invective from both individuals and a cadre of "experts" in the behavioral/psychological fields. (And here I thought these "people specialists" were supposed to teach others how to control vituperative responses!) Taken as a group these written complaints all *sided with the pest*—not the victims of intolerable behavior.

One male correspondent took the incident as a chance to unleash a jeremiad against the "corporate mind and its disdain for human growth." He was incensed that this cold corporate office didn't "warm up" enough to investigate whether the pest needed professional counseling and provide him with same. Apparently he feels strongly that a business organization has an obligation to help employees solve their personal problems. In much the same vein (viciously) a female correspondent denounced the two victims as "petty," "small potatoes" and "ignoramuses" because they didn't "enlarge their circle to include another who is a good, well-intentioned worker." By signing herself, "Had it with the likes of you," I could only conclude that *she* is an identical pest who has been similarly ostracized by annoyed co-workers.

The interpersonal-relations specialists were far more voluable—pages upon pages of the "proper" solution descended upon me and the magazine. As far as I know the alternative suggestions might be suitable somewhere, but without exception these critics did not understand the on-the-job situation so clearly outlined by "Exasperated." For instance, one thought the writer was upset at the insensitivity of her boss, not the pest, so the expert recommended that the victims "give the manager a detailed report outlining the loss of time and production or profit losses caused by this disruptive co-worker, obligating him to intervene." Clearly this human-relations specialist doesn't understand organizational structures or else she'd know that the power lines flow in the opposite direction—that subordinates cannot "obligate" a boss to do anything; it's the other way around. Furthermore, this particular boss had already refused to get involved and had "delegated" the responsibility to the parties concerned.

Despite the boss's clear-cut unwillingness to become entangled (his right by virtue of his position, no matter how unwise from a managerial standpoint), the boss became the recipient of tons of unsolicited advice from helpful academics and behavioral psychologists. The gist of most of it was to turn the manager into a pop-psychologist who should recognize the "cycle of aggression and counter-aggression" going on here or to realize that "no matter what the pestered says, she enjoys the adulation" and her complaint is a form of "bragging in disguise." Having neatly twisted the whole situation to *blame the victims*, the humanist experts proceeded to outline the interminable process the manager must follow to evade "taking sides" and to avoid "any pangs of guilt or regret," should (presumably) the time ever come when a managerial *decision* is inescapable. What the various sociological systems had in common was time: The various processes required enormous amounts of time and incessant meetings with the affected individuals on the part of the manager. None of the experts seemed to be aware that managers as well as subordinates have a primary claim on their time—to get the department's work accomplished.

Of course the commercial assertiveness trainers were very upset. As one of them pointed out (although not in these terms), their bread-and-butter depends on attracting attendees to their seminars where they'll teach men and women how to handle this type of problem without committing the sin of aggressiveness. Obviously they don't subscribe to my pragmatic approach because they fear I "am guiding many down a path which leads to failure." They're entitled to their opinion, but it's not necessarily sound.

At the end of this deluge, a short handwritten note on typical office-memo stationery appeared in the mail. It merits a place in my "most welcome" correspondence file:

*Dear Betty Harragan:*
*You probably appreciate feedback so I wanted to thank you. My assistant and I found that many of your observations were on target,*

*and we've put into practice some of the advice, such as giving this pest a project when he wanders into one of our offices, coffee cup in hand.*

*Perhaps the only area in which your assessment of the situation was off base was your suggestion that we have formed a "two-group" and resent intruders. Actually, my assistant is probably the most gregarious person in our headquarters office, with many friends among management and secretaries, and we are not at all close socially even though we work together often. Her gregariousness, however, may be as much a reason for this man's belief that he can pester us as anything else in our behavior. You got us to analyze our behavior with him and to have a constructive dialogue rather than a "bitch session." Thanks for your help.*

*Exasperated*

# "ME TARZAN, YOU JANE"

*Dear Betty Harragan:*

*I had a conversation with a male colleague last week that provided me with a "moment of truth" crisis in my career. This man approached me with a "Me Tarzan, you Jane" attitude and announced that my work load originally had been his before I joined the department eighteen months ago. He demanded that I give him back these assignments because budget cuts have curtailed his company-travel schedule and he now has time on his hands. The move left me with no work load, but I rationalized that we were essentially fighting over a few sheets of paper that represented some authority mantle to him; basically he wanted his toys back. I let him have his work back but I was bothered, since I am his peer professional, not his subordinate. So I dared ask the deadly question.*

*"Mike," I said, "let's be honest. It seems that my very presence here disturbs you. You and our boss have always claimed that I don't work well with others, that I'm too aggressive or pushy, and that's your excuse for isolating me. Tell me, do I threaten you that much?" He paused, took a deep breath and answered, "Yes."*

*It so happens that sexism is growing more blatant by the minute in my company (a pharmaceutical firm). With the demise of the ERA there was a feeling that it's back to the gentlemen's clubs, and the sooner the better. Our company resembles a James Thurber battlefield, with the guys paranoid about losing their jobs in the present economy. I've noticed that other women are effectively excluded from their work groups just as I am.*

*We women are products of good educations, bright and ambitious, out there running with the ball, reading the management books, dressing properly, thinking corporately—and have temporarily put our ovaries in formaldehyde in order to "make it." Well, it isn't working. The fast track appears to have a serious bottleneck. Must women continually go (as I'm doing) from company to company to make career jumps whenever blocked by discrimination? "Out of the frying pan, into the fire" career planning. Who wants to start a job knowing you're going to leave at the end of eighteen months because the same scenario repeats itself? We women have more than a problem on our hands—it's like a terminal sociological disease. Is there any help?*

*—Stalemated*

Dear Stalemated:

From the tone of your letter, I can guess your age—you are 30, give or take a year. The clue was your admission that the recent conversation with a male peer precipitated a "moment of truth" crisis in your thinking. Indeed, the forthright nature of the conversation localizes both you and your colleague in the generation that graduated from college and started work during the mid-1970s, when affirmative action was at its peak and spurred the hiring of women on an equal basis with men. (Older women, who launched careers before equal-opportunity laws, would not initiate such a frank discussion because they'd know beforehand what answers to expect; they've heard them often enough.)

Nevertheless, you were courageous to face the issue head-on. It's one thing to intellectually suspect that you are a threat to male colleagues, but quite another to experience the emotional jolt of hearing that truth straight from the men's mouths. Many women your age are first encountering gender discrimination as the ravages of the economy force cutbacks on practically all companies. Yours is not the only big corporation where men are paranoid about losing their jobs. Under the circumstances, it's not surprising that they turn on female co-workers and try all kinds of tricks to drive the women down or out.

You have been a victim of this pervasive discrimination for some time but apparently didn't identify it. For one thing, your boss is clearly in cahoots with your male peer or peers in setting up an all-boys wall to keep you out. Their approach is classic: You can't get along with others (i.e., them) and you're too aggressive (you should be meek and subservient, the way women are supposed to be). This kind of accusation is calculated to make you feel unsure, unworthy, incompetent or unfeminine. It's a form of burrowing from within, since many women have fought hard to overcome those very feelings of insecurity and it doesn't take much to revivify ingrained self-doubts. On the surface, you don't sound as if you've fallen into their trap by letting these criticisms get to you. Or have you?

How do you really explain your inclination to cave in to your male peer's outrageous request to give him back his old work? Granted, you fought about it, but then you "rationalized" that this brouhaha involved only "a few sheets of paper." Not so. Those routine assignments constituted your entire work load, the reason you were hired a year and a half ago. Presumably that is the date when your colleague accepted the more interesting assignments that took him on the road and, he gambled, afforded him independence and visibility—good expedients for moving ahead faster. Unfortunately for him, his great hopes were shattered by the recession, and now he's sitting around the office doing nothing. He can surely see that his situation is vulnerable (he's lucky to be still on the payroll). So he looks around and sees you busily occupied at his previous job and gets a bright idea: He'll be safe for a time if he can just manage to get his old job back.

It was a mark of colossal nerve to approach you with that proposition, and I bet he'd never dare suggest it to another man (he'd risk a punch in the nose). But he gambled again, this time on his gut instinct that because you're a female you won't see what he's up to and will gracefully succumb to his demands. (That accounts for your perception of the "Me Tarzan, you Jane" histrionics.) He revealed his basically low opinion of women's intelligence by assuming that you'd (a) be eager to "help" him as women traditionally do, (b) be too dumb to realize he was transferring his vulnerability to you, (c) be too overwhelmed by his male superiority to object.

For whichever reason, he guessed right. You voluntarily handed him your job and thereby proved to him (and to your boss) that self-styled bright women are suckers who can be manipulated with the most transparent of tricks. In a sense, you faced your first minor skirmish on behalf of your legitimate job rights, and you turned tail and ran. Why didn't you stick up for yourself? Those earlier women who battled valiantly to open the job doors to give you and your generation the opportunities you enjoy expect a little gumption from the beneficiaries. The least you could have done was laughed and ignored him. He's a peer, an equal; he has no power over you or your decision, and no authority whatsoever to coopt your assignments. I imagine the guy was stunned to be so easily victorious when his only weapon was bravado.

You can be sure that the tale of his bloodless foray to recapture his old job will be embroidered hilariously as it gets passed around in the old boys' locker room. He may even be tagged for promotion on the strength of his ingenuity at solving excess-personnel problems through wit and daring. But this bodes no good for you and other women. You have simply reinforced all the worst stereotypes about women in business, especially the ones that say women don't have what it takes to be successful, that they can't withstand the slightest adversity or belligerence. Or worse yet, that they aren't competitive. You were inveigled into a typical corporate game ploy where all the odds were in your favor but you didn't so much as lift your racquet. Even if you were planning to quit anyway, you've left a residue as an ineffectual player—and who wants such a teammate on their side?

Despite your inability to cope with sexism (or see how you contribute to it), you're right that it is becoming more blatant with each passing day. Not only failure to pass the ERA, but also the moribund state of equal-employment enforcement plus the no-growth economy have conspired to remove the pressure on employers. Consequently, you may find that your 1970s' pattern of job-hopping to get ahead will not prove as effective in the 1980s. If you have a high-demand skill you may get jobs, but you won't move ahead—you'll just get a duplicate job at different companies. That is precisely what happened in the 1950s and 1960s when sex discrimination was legal and accepted; highly educated, competent women had no choice but to stay in the same dead-end job all their lives, or to shuttle from company to company doing the same things at almost the same salary but in a slightly different environment.

Yes, Virginia, there was a Santa Claus in the 1970s who passed out expensive job presents to good little girls, but now you're grown up and can't count on such largesse. Unless women like you, who progressed through the professional workforce during the past ten years, take a stand and combat entrenched sex discrimination wherever it occurs, the gains of the 1970s may be relegated to the history books. Your male associates called you aggressive. They've gotta be kidding.

## OFFICE UNIFORMS

*Dear Betty Harragan:*

*I work for a small southern bank with sixteen employees—twelve women (of whom I'm the only officer) and four men (three of whom are officers). The women are required to wear uniforms furnished by the bank. Admittedly, these don't look like uniforms except that we are all required to wear the same blouse and skirt on a given day. The men, however, are not required to wear matching blazers or any other semblance of a uniform. The top two men wear suits most days, but the other two wear what they want; usually the third officer wears a dress shirt and the nonofficer wears a sports shirt. I've complained about this discriminatory situation to the powers that be, but no one takes me seriously because they claim I can't come up with a better solution, or they just dismiss me as the resident "libber." I seem to be the only woman here who considers herself a career professional and wants to get somewhere in the power structure of this bank. In fact, I expect to be promoted to a senior officer within the year; then I will have jurisdiction over uniforms! Should I start laying a groundwork to convince management that female dissatisfaction with uniforms could be eliminated by making all men wear matching blazers or suits every day?*

*Isolated*

Dear Isolated:

You bring up a knotty issue. The subject of appropriate clothing for business wear has endless ramifications that run deep into personal, psychological, cultural and class sensibilities, as well as business necessity.

Your anticipated responsibility for company uniforms is not an enviable one; most managers try to evade this hot potato if they can. Nevertheless, it is a subject that must be handled in a well-run office because the clothing worn by employees has a definite influence on the working environment and, often, on the efficiency of the operation, especially in a situation like yours where practically all employees deal with—or are visible to—customers. You are wise to be thinking about this problem in advance because a new solution is nowhere near as simple as the one you propose.

Apparently you have already suggested that the "uniform rule" should be extended to males as well as females. This approach could easily get you dismissed as a women's "libber" because it presents the problem purely in female/male terms. In essence, as you were told, your narrow focus is not useful because you aren't coming up with a practical substitute for current management policy. It's a case where both you and management are right, up to a point, but neither of you have fully analyzed the gist of your disagreement.

Your company's management made a sound business decision in establishing a homogeneous look for its employees so that customers can easily identify bank personnel. I suspect the chosen outfits fall in the neat, innocuous, unadorned category, because banks have a strong tradition of maintaining a serious, conservative image. Your company wisely followed through with the decision to furnish the main articles of clothing it insisted employees wear.

This eliminated objections from low-paid employees that they couldn't afford expensive special clothing just to benefit their employer.

So far so good for your company's dress policy—but then something went off the beam and you saw it immediately: The dress code applied to women only. You correctly attributed the result to discrimination against women, but you have to analyze the components of dissimilar treatment before you can recommend an acceptable new policy. Look closely at the employee composition: eleven females, one male in clerical or support functions; one female, three males in officer positions. This is the first breakdown that's important—*job levels*—not gender. Mandated dress codes generally apply to nonexecutive (nonexempt) employees; officials, managers and other exempt employees are expected to conform through voluntary adoption of company dress standards.

It so happens in your bank (like most others) that the nonexempt jobs are held almost exclusively by women. Thus, the uniform rule applies almost exclusively to women, not because they are female but because they work at these jobs. The lone male obviously posed a problem to management so they chose to ignore him and let him wear what he wanted. That is clearly sex discrimination because one employee of a dozen is being treated differently for no reason except gender. Any new policy you propose must include this specific male (and any other men who are subsequently hired for these jobs) with the women. He must be provided with company shirts that match the female blouses in style and color for the given days. He belongs in the "uniform" crowd because he holds an equivalent job; gender can have nothing to do with it.

Now we come to the crucial separation that affects you—the officer rank. Your idea that *all* men should be ordered to wear matching blazers will never be tolerated because that would put male officers on the same job level as any male clerical/support staff workers. Don't mention that idea again because it will only antagonize senior executives or, at best, make them wonder if you really understand how business operates. Banks, large or small, are the same as any kind of corporation; they are hierarchical structures modeled after the military. Their executives are even called officers, just like the army—and in the army, a lieutenant or captain does not wear a private's uniform (or vice versa). There is a vast difference between officers and enlisted troops, not only in title but in authority, responsibility and status symbols like uniforms.

Your superiors laugh at your "solutions" to the uniform issue because, by dressing all males alike, you are saying that everybody should wear a private's uniform so that everybody appears "equal." Worse yet, you are insinuating that all male officers look indistinguishable from the newest clerk. This is manifestly unrealistic because business organizations are not democracies; they are layered pyramids with successions of job levels or classifications. Women particularly (but lots of young men, too) hate to recognize these class separations, probably because women are usually in the lowest categories. But men in the higher levels are acutely aware of job-class distinctions.

Understandably women resent dictation of what they can wear to work because they instinctively sense that this labels them low echelon. Sometimes it does but that's not the uniform's fault; there are many sound business reasons for uniformity of dress and not all uniforms are low echelon—look at airline pilots, for example. If a certain uniform goes with a given job there is nothing to do about it except get promoted to a higher level where a more prestigious uniform (voluntary or involuntary) delineates the higher classification.

You have done just that, but your company's discriminatory dress policy almost negates your promotion. By being forced to wear the uniform furnished by the bank only to female employees, you are still being classified in the nonexempt ranks where that uniform is mandated. The rest of the staff as well as all the customers assume you aren't *really* an officer because you don't display the important status symbol, an officer's uniform. This implicit demotion of your rank was probably not intentional; management couldn't figure out how to handle the odd female officer any more than they could cope with the odd male clerk—so they handily ignored the two exceptions and are leaving themselves wide open to a clear-cut sex discrimination charge. As the sole female officer, you are being treated noticeably different from your male peers—for no discernible reason other than gender.

You have two powerful reasons to continue your campaign for a nondiscriminatory dress code. When you're in charge of the uniform policy, you have to make sure it conforms to the law; before that, you have to ensure that you are given the proper respect for your position. You must not wear a teller's uniform if you want respect as an officer. You have to acknowledge that you belong to the upper levels in your company hierarchy and assert your right to voluntary control over the clothes you wear to work. Perhaps the fastest way to bring this issue to a head is to act instead of arguing. Start coming to work in business outfits that you have decided conform to the "look" adopted by male officers.

Take your cue from the two men who wear suits. You needn't copy them exactly but you should adopt a long-sleeved jacket outfit that sets you apart from the blouse-and-skirt teller uniform. Also watch the colors so you do not duplicate the uniform colors; again, follow those two senior male officers. If they wear dark colors, you wear dark (at least until you establish your point and are perceived as their peer). Since bankers are generally subdued in dress, do not wear any jewelry beyond a watch and a ring, and no fancy footware like sandals, clogs or ankle-straps! Conservative good taste is the image you want to convey.

Thanks to feminist attorneys who keep tabs on precedent-setting court decisions, I subsequently found out this case has been litigated. In *Carroll v. Talman Federal Savings and Loan Association of Chicago,* August 21, 1979, the United States Court of Appeals, Seventh Circuit, reversed the District Court and ruled that the employer's dress policy, which required female employees to wear color-coordinated uniforms but allowed men in the same positions to wear personal business attire, was a violation of Title VII of the Civil Rights Act because it discriminated against women.

Clearly, this was a hard-fought case (the next step would be the Supreme Court) so I naturally wondered why the employer refused to conciliate the issue, as it could have done several times, but preferred to fight through the court system to maintain its disparate treatment of male and female employees. I felt reasonably sure that the text would yield some fascinating nuggets for women on the volatile subject of appropriate business clothing—and I wasn't disappointed. I asked my friend Joan Bertin, staff counsel at the Women's Rights Project of the American Civil Liberties Union to send me a copy of the decision (604 F.2d 1028 7thCir. 1979); it's a beauty as an unexpected contribution to the "Dress for Success" literature.

First, the legal background. Title VII laywers generally refer to personal appearance matters as "the grooming cases." Nobody likes them, because the issues get beclouded by controversies over "reasonable business necessity" and everybody's subjective, emotional reaction to "what's proper" in clothes or grooming. Consequently many complaints don't get far; those that do are usually decided in favor of the employer on the basis that slight deviations between male and female standards are inevitable in the area of looks. Actually, most of the litigated cases were brought by men who charged sex discrimination when they were required to wear a tie or have short hair, while women weren't forced to do either. Invariably these charges are dismissed (as late as 1977) as not violations of Title VII.

In *Carroll* the situation was different. Talman Savings required its 525 female employees (tellers, officers and managerial personnel) to wear a two-piece uniform assembled from five basic items: color-coordinated skirt or slacks and a choice of jacket, tunic or vest. "There is no question," the Court said, "that the various combinations depict uniforms"—and produced photographs to prove it. In contrast, the 150 male employees (also tellers, officers and managerial personnel) were permitted to wear business suits or business-type sports jackets and pants and ties, or leisure suits with a suitable shirt and tie. Any woman who showed up for work without her uniform was suspended, except on the last Tuesday of each month when the uniforms had to be cleaned, and the week between Christmas and New Years.

The company claimed that female employees liked the uniform and had a Career Ensemble Committee that voted on the style, color and supplier of the garments. Its dress code, if discriminatory, was reasonably necessary to the operation of its business because:

> Dress competition among women is reduced and they do not have to be concerned about wearing something that is appropriate business attire because the career ensemble is acceptable. Dress competition exists among women employees on glamour days but in the case of men employees there is little difficulty getting them to ad-

here to the dress and grooming code requirements . . . there is little dress competition among male employees.

Company attorneys elaborated on this theme in oral arguments:

> The selection of attire, of clothing on the part of women is not a matter of business judgment. It is a matter of taste, a matter of what the other women are wearing, what fashion is currently. When we get into that realm, problems develop. Somehow, the women who have excellent business judgment somehow follow the fashion, and the slit-skirt fashion which is currently prevalent. . . . They tend to follow those fashions and they don't seem to equate that with a matter of business judgment.

The Appeals Court didn't fall for these arguments as the District Court had. It said such open admissions were based on "offensive stereotypes" and assumed "that women cannot be expected to exercise good judgment in choosing business apparel, whereas men can." The Court quickly noted that "career ensemble" was merely a euphemism for "uniform" since the days when women were exempt from wearing it were referred to as "glamour days." (Incidentally, the personnel director had testified that women never wore improper business attire on those days.) The Court concluded: "Moreover, the disparate treatment is demeaning to women. While there is nothing offensive about uniforms per se, when some employees are uniformed and others not there is a natural tendency to assume that the uniformed women have lesser professional status than their male colleagues attired in normal business clothes."

Another little item brought down the wrath of this court—discrimination in compensation. The company allegedly furnished the original two-piece uniform to women (after that, they had to pay for cleaning, upkeep, replacement or additional pieces) but the company then withheld income tax from their wages for the cost of the uniform—thereby treating the uniform as income to women employees! Instead of these separate, sex-based dress codes, the Court listed permissable alternatives the company could adopt:

1  Legitimately require women to wear "appropriate business attire," such as businesslike skirts or pants and a vest and jacket, as in the case of men.

2  Make the uniform optional. If women liked it so much, that should present no problem.

3  Require comparable male employees to wear some sort of uniform, as numerous other banks and savings institutions do. "Title VII does not require that uniforms be abolished but that similarly situated employees be treated in an equal manner."

But that isn't the end of Mary M. Carroll's fascinating decision. Circuit Judge Pell violently disagreed with his colleagues and issued a dissent that was almost as long as the majority opinion. He concurred with the lower court, which had ruled this situation not discriminatory, and agreed with the employer's policy for an ingenious reason all his own. If you ever think that the clothes you wear to work—regardless of job level or occupation—do not arouse violent emotions, think again. As you read his remarkable diatribe, remember that this is word-for-word (and comma for comma) from a most official document: the *legal* opinion of one of the senior federal judges in our land.

With this decision of this court, Big Brother—or perhaps in this case, Big Sister—has encroached, in my opinion, farther than the Congress intended or authorized into the domain of private enterprise, or what remains of that concept . . . simply to respond to the emotional complaint of one disgruntled employee. . . .

The majority opinion categorizes the clothing women are required to wear at work as uniforms but refers to that which men must wear as customary business attire. These characterizations ignore the fact of life that men's customary business attire has never really advanced beyond the status of being a uniform. True there have been variations from time to time probably mainly attributable to the desire of clothiers to stay in business—there have been wide and narrow lapels, cuffed and cuffless trousers, different colored shirts which are ordinarily substantially covered by jackets, some splashes of color in neckties, a choice of four-in-hands or bow ties,

nonvested and vested suits, a choice of belted or beltless or sus-
pender-supported trousers, ankle-length or over-the-calf hosiery,
pleated and nonpleated trousers, three-button or two-button jackets
and even occasionally in daring moments a pleated-back jacket. In
the most innovative soaring from the nest of uniformity that I can
recall in recent decades someone introduced the so-called leisure
suit which upon any fair analysis itself resembles a uniform. Men,
of course, do have a choice of materials and colors in their suit, or
sport jacket and slacks outfits, but I am not aware that lurid colors
would qualify as "customary business attire," any more than would
one of the bizarre assemblages worn by a modern rock singer.

On the other hand, women have had a wide range of nonuni-
formity, of recent vintage being the slit skirt and a few years earlier
the mini which often barely qualified as a skirt. High boots have
alternated with spike heels and sandals. The dresses, or blouses and
skirts which are not covered by outer jackets as in the situation of
men, are multicolored and multipatterned. Women frequently now
wear slacks, an accoutrement in previous years regarded as being
the exclusive province of the male.

In sum, customary business attire for the men employees of Talman seems to me to confine these employees in a uniform to the
same extent as the Talman dress code does for women, in each case
in reality not so much for the purpose of requiring a uniform but
for the purpose of achieving a uniformity of businesslike attire. One
only has to observe people on the way to business jobs on the side-
walks of Chicago to be aware of the essential uniformity of male
garb and the lack of that uniformity among women.

I recognize that the favorite putting-down remark that is resorted
to when anyone is so bold as to delineate actual factual differences
between men and women—in this case, the clothing that they customarily wear—is to accuse the person of indulging in stereotyping.
If what I have written about the difference of clothing styles between the sexes be stereotyping, I will borrow an oft-quoted phrase
from one of our forebears . . . "Make the most of it."

A second factor in the present case is that the career ensembles
women are required to wear are not unattractive in style, inferior in
quality, ill-fitting, or uncomfortable such that they would cause
embarrassment or be considered demeaning. . . . As I stated at the
outset of this dissent the dress standards applied to both men and

women result in ordinary business attire although the rules are se-
mantically different. This difference in form, although not in sub-
stance, is not sufficient to constitute a substantial burden for
females in the enjoyment of their jobs. Again, we would have a
quite different case if, for example, the female employees of a savings and loan association were required to wear dehumanizing or
uncomfortable clothing, or drab unstylish outfits, or any other attire which by the acceptable female dress norms of the time would
be considered as embarrassing or demeaning to the wearer while
male employees were only required to wear conventional business
suits. [Note: The majority opinion said: "We do not think the personal taste of this Court is relevant to the rights involved in this
appeal, but we are quite certain that there is room for differences of
opinion on the sartorial excellence of the uniforms."]

Finally, I regard the . . . fact that women have to pay income
tax on the first outfit provided to them without cost as nit-picking.
When the men buy their business wear apparel they pay the full
price without any tax deduction, the amount being far more substantial than the income tax based on the cost of the clothing received by the women. Women, of course, have to keep their
ensembles in repair and cleaned. So do the men. Any replacements
must be paid for by the women. Likewise the men must pay for the
clothing they wear.

Opponents of the Equal Rights Amendment have argued that its
adoption would be followed by extreme applications bordering on
the ridiculous where no meaningful discrimination exists. The result reached by the majority opinion in the application of the stat-
ute I can only regard as adding strength to that argument.

Any more questions about the propriety of slit skirts?

## RACISM OR SEXISM?

*Dear Betty Harragan:*
*I am a black woman engineer employed by a public agency where*
*I'm in charge of specific technical contracts. My authority to accept*
*or reject certain designs or pieces of equipment is frequently overrid-*
*den by higher management in favor of men with opposing view-*

*points. The environment here is predominantly white male and heavy on retired military officers. I present my opinions in a straightforward manner, backed by technical proof and documentation, but I'm called "a bitch" for trying to remain objective. When I point out errors of operation or ill-advised suggestions from other engineers, I'm accused of not being a "team player." The politics of this organization call for a get-the-job-done philosophy with a don't-rock-the-boat mentality. The rationale is that many of these people will meet again on future engineering projects, so they refuse to openly oppose each other. I'm always on the defensive because, deep down, they believe a black and/or a woman doesn't know enough to be here, let alone dissent. Even when I'm right they gang up and make me wrong, in effect, by covering up mistakes of the men. How can I get equal treatment and equal pay without alienating everybody? The tactics that work for whites don't work well for blacks.*
                                                                    *Paranoid*


Dear Paranoid:

At the risk of alienating a lot of blacks, I'm going to say that racism may be the least of your problems. That doesn't mean I'm insensitive to the double discrimination faced by minority women, but the elements of racism and sexism must be assigned their proper weight before you can figure out logical solutions.

You are clearly carrying the burden of being seen as the "two-fer" in your agency—the token female who is also black and thus satisfies (in one person) the absolute minimal sex and race requirements of Equal Employment Opportunity laws. But in one respect, your gender-race combination is not a handicap; those are the characteristics that got you the job in the first place. Add to those a third sterling qualification—your prestigious engineering degree. As you surely know, only about three percent of graduate engineers are female, and black females are a fragment of that minuscule total. In other words, you must be one of the most sought-after professionals in the country.

If you are serious about not getting equal pay, merely walk in and ask for it. Don't negotiate, don't argue; just mention the subject. Your affirmative-action properties are so rare and valuable that you could command *higher* pay than comparable white men, without lifting a finger. Don't be afraid to capitalize on native and earned advantages you have.

However, I think you are right to be concerned about equal pay in the future when, as you anticipate, salary will be tied to recognition and performance. So here we get to the nub of your problem: How to gain recognition within an alien group whose members automatically treat you like an idiot outsider. Instead of concentrating on your differences (race and sex), think about the strong bond you share with co-workers—your profession. As an occupational group, engineers are purported to be independent thinkers, individualists, nonconformists, perfectionists. You sound as if you fit that description very well or you wouldn't have gotten where you are today. No doubt you are an excellent engineer, both in fact and by temperament.

But you must remember that you work with a crowd of equally self-aggrandizing, if not pompous, experts, most of whom are a good deal older and more experienced than you (though not necessarily more capable). Over the years, they have learned a hard lesson that you don't yet appreciate; namely, that there is much more to business success than technical proficiency. The ultimate objective is to get the job done with the least amount of flack (certainly in a public agency). That's the very necessity that you rebel against, so you keep hammering away at "objective" facts and remind everyone of their past mistakes in not listening to you. Such arrogant behavior wouldn't win you any friends even if you were white and male; it smacks too much of the schoolroom pest who keeps trying to prove he's the smartest kid in the class.

Without compromising your own talents or ability, I'd suggest you become more flexible in judging others' decisions. Even though you have strong reservations on some point, it's possible their approach may have some merits you overlooked. Present your conclusions, of course, but go down to defeat gracefully if you are overridden. Engineers are by no means infallible, judging by the calamitous flops of some superstars who've designed buses, buildings, subways, arenas, automobiles, bridges, rockets, etc.

I think you'll find that accommodation tactics work well for blacks and women who want to progress in a white male environment. If adapting to their system doesn't gain you credibility, *then* you know that sex and/or race bias is operating.

Incidentally, with your four-star credentials, I can't help wondering why you're working for a public agency. You'd probably feel more comfortable and have a much brighter future in private industry—once you've learned how to function smoothly in a complex working environment.

In light of my trepidation about alienating blacks (whites evaluating racism are legitimately suspect), I am happy to report that I got no criticism from black women professionals. This column evoked considerable response but on an issue so divorced from racism or sexism that it deserves—and gets—equal treatment in the following section.

Black women engineers and scientists agreed that my advice was on target and a couple asked for more attention to black women's problems inasmuch as black women with sterling qualifications are widely represented in professional ranks. One respondent, however, (black or non-black is unclear) brought up an attitude that was once quite widespread; it should be dispensed with because it has dangerous implications for career-oriented women.

As a psychotherapist for women I am concerned with the implications of "accommodation tactics" to progress in a white male environment. You put Paranoid in a classic double-bind by failing to point out that "the system," by definition, operates on underlying assumptions about power, authority, expertise and legitimacy that are definitely race/sex issues. By suggesting "adaptation" to this system, you failed to show her that the consequence of not alienating herself from co-workers will be alienating herself from *herself* as a competent black woman. You cannot do justice to her request without presenting the pros and cons of "accommodating" so she can objectively decide whether it's worth it, and at what cost to her self-esteem.

While no doubt sincere, this convoluted reasoning is nonsense. *Of course* "the system" is racist and sexist. It got that way by excluding women, blacks, and other minorities. This is known as systemic discrimination on the basis of race, creed, color, ethnic origin, or sex and is the practice outlawed by Title VII of the Civil Rights Act. Hundreds of thousands of committed women and minority men fought (and are still fighting) for access to that "system"—the American economic system. To insinuate that a highly qualified individual should spurn an opportunity to infiltrate this economic system (and eventually make valuable contributions to it) is to fly in the face of the concept of "equal opportunity" and a fully integrated workforce. The true danger to Paranoid's self-esteem will come about if she fails to be successful; but that need not happen if she learns to function effectively in complex working environments.

## GOVERNMENT ENGINEERS CHIME IN

If I can stretch a point and consider myself a "co-worker" of the myriad women in hundreds of occupations with whom I carry on a steady dialogue, then this correspondence is an example of how we can learn from each other. I have never worked in the government sector and my ignorance showed up in a final statement I made in the foregoing problem of the black woman engineer: I insinuated that a high achiever might be more successful if she got out of the public sector and aimed for private industry.

I was unaware how deeply that comment offended a substantial segment of working women—those who have chosen to build their careers in federal, state or local government. Thank goodness they let me know, in no uncertain terms, that they resented any implication that government service attracts less competent, less qualified professionals. Two agreed to use their real names and current job titles because they are so proud of their accomplishments.

I was distressed to realize my words could be taken as a disparagement of government officials because I had no such intention. Far from it, since I have had close association with women who hold administrative posts in various government agencies and am keenly aware of their difficulties in gaining recognition for their exceptional ability and performance. What I did not know is that dedicated public servants are very sensitive on this issue because they are frequently put down and patronized by outsiders (like me) who ask why they work for the government, as if to say, "If you're so good, how come you're not in private industry?" In my own defense I have to admit I was thinking primarily of career options that an ambitious young engineer might not have considered. She was probably earning a much lower salary than her desirable credentials could presently command in the private sector. Money alone, however, is a very short-sighted approach to long-range career planning. Therefore I am indebted to those busy executives who, from their own experience, put the case for government service as a career option into its proper perspective.

*Dear Betty Harragan:*

*As a black female professional, I am proud of my achievements, the agency for which I work and the people with whom I work. At a Brookings Institution seminar for government executives on business policy and operations, I took heart from statements made by Mel Horwitch, professor of business administration at M.I.T.'s Sloan School of Management. He said that in many instances, particularly in the realm of strategic decision-making, private industry would do well to learn from the example of government managers.*

*The myths that public employment is inevitably "second-class" or that the public sector employs only those who can't make it in the private sector, are just that—myths. Some of us choose to remain in the public sector because we want to work in an environment where our contributions can make a difference and where we see tangible evidence every day that the work we do benefits millions of people. It is a disservice to public employees to perpetuate tired, outworn untruths.*

> *Sharon Smith Holston*
> *Deputy Associate Commissioner*
> *For Management and Operations*
> *U.S. Food and Drug Administration*
> *Rockville, MD*

*Dear Betty Harragan:*

*Now, more than ever, it is vital that dedicated professionals, particularly engineers, join government service. Engineering projects of enormous magnitude with tremendous impact on people and on America's future are being proposed by government officials. It is important that there be competent voices within the government to plan projects well, to stimulate debate, and to seek competent firms to carry them out. Comparatively little engineering work is actually performed by the government today. Most design and construction work is done by contractors—private industry. But it is government engineers who assure that government contractors do quality work. Private industry follows through on government plans. Which is more important—the idea or the product?*

*I am an engineer with bachelor's and master's degrees in civil engineering and a B.A. in social welfare. I have been in government service—municipal and federal—for ten years. Presently I am responsible for numerous multimillion dollar projects. Private industry is better for engineers in one regard only—money. If an engineer's career goal is to make as much money as possible, by all means follow the route to private industry. Recognizing its inability to compete in this area, government has established special salary scales for entry-level engineers but salaries for middle or top level engineering positions are not comparable.*

*From my own experience, I would like to add some points to help Paranoid function more smoothly in her complex working environment. One of the great faults of engineers is to look at an issue strictly from a technical viewpoint. Today an engineer must be aware of all ramifications that a project could trigger—environmental or social impacts, for example. In Paranoid's situation, it would be beneficial to know beforehand what her "opponents'" objections are and why. With that information she could formulate alternatives, determine pros and cons, and solidify her viewpoint by taking these factors into account. For example, if a project called for constructing a highway though the center of a small town, townspeople may object vehemently. The route might be technically and economically sound but the impact on the people could be devastating. Understanding this and realizing that the project could be delayed by residents, it might be better to think about alternatives.*

*Another thing Paranoid might do is talk to her "opponents" before a meeting to find out what their objections are. Since her colleagues have been in the profession for many years, she might ask them for advice based on their experience. In this way, they could get to know her (and vice versa) in a nonconfrontational situation. She could make suggestions or ask questions without putting her opponents in a position where they have to defend their records in front of colleagues. She should not, of course, compromise her ethics in the name of teamwork, which would be a disservice to herself and her profession.*

R. Shirlene Clemence
Chief, Engineering Resources Management
Division
Karlsruhe Directorate of Engineering and Housing
APO NY 09164

*Dear Betty Harragan:*
*As an engineering-related professional with a B.A. in chemistry, an M.S. in environmental science, and considerable M.B.A. credits, I relate strongly to the problems discussed. Government work, although frequently frustrating, is stimulating and interesting. You are where it's at, so to speak—involved in writing, enforcing, carrying out, and influencing the formation of policies, regulations and procedures. Your implication about the poor reputation of government workers is unfortunate. However, it cannot be dismissed altogether as myth. Because of the nature of the system, the huge bureaucracy, and the cumbersome civil service rules, mediocrity tends to perpetuate.* Nevertheless, it does not have to be assumed in every case.

*Those of us who were first to break the sex barriers needed a thick skin and strong stomach. When I started working in state government several years ago, if there was another college-educated woman in the division of 500 I could not find her. Now there are many professional women in that division including several who, with my help, found stimulating jobs within the system which are meeting their needs very nicely.*

*Being a "first" means you are on the cutting edge and tend to remain the first as you move up the career ladder, easing the way for those who follow. Although I got tired of being on the cutting edge and decided to let someone else take over while I moved into the private sector, I am convinced that intelligent, educated women can have satisfying careers and enjoy all the terrific benefits that go with government work. By understanding the system and the personalities of people who work well within the bureaucracy, you can use it to*

*your advantage. Personality characteristics and one's personal cir-
cumstances are at least as important as credentials when making a
career choice to enter or continue in government employment.*

State Government Advocate

# JOKERS WILD

*Dear Betty Harragan:*

*I'm an electronic data processing systems analyst and the token
(only) woman in my department. The men totally and completely
isolate me, but one man has always been friendly and seemed the
nicest. One day I gathered up my courage and asked him if he'd like
to have lunch, even mentioning a restaurant we could try. The man
turned ashen, then spluttered a five-second explanation of how he
never ate lunch, etc. I said fine, if he ever did go out, let me know. I
went back to my desk (which is near my boss's office) and was
stunned to overhear this man telling our boss about my invitation
and how he wouldn't go near me with a ten-foot pole. At that, the
two of them burst into hysterical laughter. Then they both proceeded
to the office of my boss's boss, repeated the story, and all three of
them laughed hysterically. They were talking very loudly and apparently didn't care if everyone, including me, heard them. This happened at 11:59, and by 12:15 the entire finance department knew
about my asking this guy to have lunch. I am trying to live with my
rage, which I cannot describe. I am the laughing-stock of the department. Can you recommend any strategy or dialogue to alleviate my
rage?*

*Wrathful*

Dear Wrathful:

Don't try to alleviate your rage. Luxuriate in it. Anger of this
dimension is an energizing force, and that's what you need to handle the disgusting macho creeps you work with.

Legitimate anger such as you're experiencing is a dynamic,
healthy emotion. Almost any working woman can empathize with

your fury (I'm so mad I can hardly write). It's interesting that you used the phrase "live with my rage" because those are the exact words I've heard from other women after a similarly devastating experience at work. Like them, you feel as though the residue of this rage has become part of your being.

Since you are bound to be shattered by the personal insult, you may not have figured out why this incredible display of loutish behavior hit you so hard. Obviously, pesonal rejection and cruel laughter can be extremely hurtful, but they are not sufficient provocation to incite "indescribable" rage—not, that is, unless the incident exposes elemental passions that were previously hidden from consciousness. It's this, not the superficial abuse, that is fueling your anger.

Let's examine the ubiquitous prenoon ritual when an employee approaches a fellow worker about eating lunch together. The occurrence is so mundane that it's rarely dignified as an "invitation" because it is couched in cursory terms: "Ready for lunch?" "Eating with anyone today?" "How about trying the new restaurant?" Responses are just as casual: "O.K." "Good idea." "Sorry, I'm tied up." "Let's make it another day." Ordinarily there is no subterfuge in these matter-of-fact exchanges, no need for elaborate excuses or explanations.

Then a woman joins the work group as—she fervently believes—just another professional among professionals. Generally she works hard to prove herself, to earn acceptance from her peers. But gradually she perceives that she is not included in the group activities: Certain information that flows to the others never reaches her; ideas that are well received when offered by one of the men are ridiculed when she proffers them; luncheon arrangements omit her, nobody drops the informal question, "Free for lunch?"

When the isolation becomes uncomfortable, the well-meaning professional woman (especially one in the early years of her career) gets confused. She reads how-to-succeed books, attends seminars, and takes assertiveness training. She adopts the uniform skirt-suit, tries not to be too pushy or aggressive because men don't like that, but also learns she has to take the initiative to break through the seclusion. For example, if co-workers don't invite her to lunch, the logical move is to invite them to lunch. I suspect you went through

such a progression before summoning the courage to ask the "nicest" colleague to lunch.

Then look what happened!

All your expectations were torn to shreds with a vengeance. A
luncheon turndown would have been nothing in itself (a temporary
feeling of rejection, perhaps, or a realization that the nice guy is
actually a jerk). But his original shock and subsequent actions
proved to you beyond a shadow of a doubt that this episode aroused
such violent feelings of repudiation that he instantly rushed to his
boss for support and the two of them fled to a higher official for
added fortification, meanwhile loudly warning the rest of the troops
in the outer office. You actually had a rare chance to watch the
circle of male-bonding wagons draw tight—*to keep you out.*

Why should such an innocuous thing as a luncheon invitation
cause so much upheaval? You can't be any job threat to them,
certainly not to a boss two levels higher, yet he responded in the
same way as your peer and your supervisor. No, all of this unbelievable behavior on the part of the men took place because you are
a woman, a female toy who had the effrontery to think she was an
equal partner to male co-workers. Instead of being accepted as a
competent professional, a well-dressed businesswoman, a hard-
working colleague, the men perceived you solely as a sexual object.
Since you belong to this alien gender, they let you know they don't
want you on their turf.

That is the realization that burst upon you in a blinding flash of
insight. That is why your rage is boundless. You recognized that
the incident has to do with the status of women in a male-dominated work force, and that you as an individual have no control
over it. If you think you are a laughing-stock, I can only surmise
that you were one of those women who never encountered blatant
sex discrimination before. In your field, experienced professionals
are at a premium, and no doubt you believed that competence
automatically conferred acceptance regardless of gender. The
maniacal laughter you heard destroyed your innocence. For this
you can be grateful, because your anger will give you the strength
to keep fighting against the pernicious evil of female inequality.

Start on the offensive right now in your present position. Don't
skulk in a corner, but bring this incident into the light (the whole

department already knows, so you don't have to explain). Start asking every guy in the place to have lunch with you. Some may surprise you and accept because they are horrified by their bosses' despicable manners; but if any refuse, calmly say you're taking a survey to find out how many, in addition to the original trio, consider lunch hours a time for illicit sexual encounters—why else would they not want you along? Make "lunch" such a salacious word in that office that they'll be terrified to exclude you.

More important, search out other professional women in your company. Tell them the story and get it broadcast far and wide, especially the collusion of the two bosses. Word may drift to senior officials who abide by a minimal code of corporate manners and who know that laws and company policies must be obeyed, however unpalatable. You might consider going to the executive vice-president and asking for a transfer, explaining that the managers in your group are violently opposed to women co-workers. Jumping over the heads of superiors works only when you have nothing to lose, and it's virtually impossible for you to fight single-handedly against three levels of the male hierarchy.

I'm sure you've thought of quitting, but if you do you'll hand the clods in your department a clear victory without opposition, since their intention is to drive you out. Besides, things won't be much different wherever you go, just more subtle.

Beyond confronting the personal situation in your office, you also have to harness this marvelous store of anger to a much bigger wagon (or it will eat away at your insides). You want to locate other women who share your abiding fury at being scorned. Where you'll find them these days is in those organizations that have been fighting for passage of the Equal Rights Amendment. When the E.R.A. failed by three states to meet the ratification deadline of June 30, 1982, this was a public instance of women being laughed at and scorned on a monumental scale. These women (and equally enraged men) have not succumbed to their anger; like you, they have learned they cannot remain innocent and trusting any longer—as long as the Constitution reads "all men are created equal," it means that women are excluded from full rights as citizens. The E.R.A. drive has not folded, it has taken a more sophisticated direction. The identical Amendment was reintroduced in the House of Representatives as H.J. Res. 1 on January 3, 1983 and in the Senate on January 26, 1983. The campaign to win-at-last is under way in every city and state. If you do not know how to get involved, check the national office of the largest activist organizations for the name of the local chapter nearest you.

National Organization for Women
425 13th Street NW, Suite 1048
Washington, DC 20004
(202) 638-6054

National Women's Political Caucus
1411 K Street NW, Suite 1110
Washington, DC 20005
(202) 347-4456

Another new coalition was launched July 1, 1982 with 150 rallies across the country under the theme: "A New Day: Beyond ERA." It is a loosely structured consortium of close to fifty national women's, labor, religious, ethnic, civil rights and professional societies dedicated to implementing the objectives of the moribund National Plan of Action, the official recommendations from the 1977 National Women's Conference in Houston. For information on the agenda and task force papers, write:

Gene Boyer
"Beyond ERA"
218 Front Street
Beaver Dam, WI 53916

You've got the motivation and the energy—get active. You'll have the last laugh yet!

You'd think that an episode as cruel and deliberate as the laughter of these men would be unusual, wouldn't you? Not so. Tremulous voices and quivery pens testified that "the same thing happened to me." One duplicate victim astutely pointed out that there may be *no* sympathetic male executives at any level and that requests for transfers are only possible if the company is large enough to have alternatives. From her own experience, she offered additional suggestions and warnings:

> The woman should be aware of the lengths to which her bosses may be prepared to go to harass her or force her out. If she decides to stay and fight she should be aware that her supervisors may be setting her up for failure by soliciting negative comments or building a file against her. She should be prepared to defend herself by keeping a daily employment log and documenting her employers' and co-workers' behavior with respect to sex discrimination and also their possible violations of company regulations. (Naturally, she should be very careful that they don't know she is keeping this account.) She must obey all company regulations meticulously, even if her co-workers do not. For example, she must not be late even if her co-workers are habitually later than she, but those time records should go into her daily log. Of course she must document her daily accomplishments. Ideally she should get some expert legal advice and counsel, which is hard to do without some outside organizational support. Equal employment opportunity is a long-term fight.

There is another aspect to this case of the laughing hyenas that is just coming to the fore. In the Winter 1982 Research Report of the Working Women's Institute, an organization devoted to sexual harassment issues, (593 Park Avenue, New York, NY 10021, [212] 838-4240), Research Director Peggy Crull urged an expanded definition of sexual harassment. Using data from 249 women who sought crisis intervention service in 1980, she reported that fifteen percent of the cases involved harassment by co-workers or other nonbosses. Such behavior as "persistent laughing" and "lewd joking" can make the environment so tense, intolerable and hostile that numerous women were forced to leave their job. She also reported that a surprising proportion of cases involved group harassment by a number of men, including a superior, joining together to make fun of a female co-worker. The research study concluded that there are important forms of sexual harassment which are more insidious and hidden than the clearly understood situation of a boss demanding sexual favors from a powerless subordinate (see Chapter 8).

The implications of these findings for women workers is to understand the many complex ways in which sexual harassment operates to damage women's self-esteem and undercut their motivation and career ambitions. As is so often the case with women's job problems, what starts out to be an obnoxious case of isolating and excluding a female co-worker may turn out to be a new direction in interpreting illegal male behavior toward women associates.

This possibility only underscores my original advice to let top management know about the incident and publicize the behavior far and wide within the company ranks.

# CHAPTER FOUR

# Confusing Categories

## WHO'S "EXEMPT" AND "NONEXEMPT"

*Dear Betty Harragan:*
*You occasionally describe jobs as "exempt" or "nonexempt," and that raises an issue that has been bothering me for some time. As far as I know, our company has no pay scale for salaried employees. Would I be within my legal rights to ask to be shown one? I once saw the president's secretary working on an organization chart and asked if I could see it, but she refused, saying it was not allowed. I started my job in a manufacturing firm four years ago as a junior accountant. After one year I was given a little more responsibility, a tiny raise, and a title change to accountant. (I have a two-year associate degree); yet my supervisor regards, treats, and refers to me as an account clerk. All our office and administrative personnel are classified as either exempt or nonexempt, and I understand that one of the criteria for determining the classification is the percentage of time spent on routine tasks. It seems to me there is a large gray area where personnel directors can sway the determination of these criteria to suit their own purposes. Could you enlighten me?*

*Provoked*

Dear Provoked:

More women than ever admit are as confused as you are about the meaning of the terms "exempt" and "nonexempt." Worse yet, department managers and personnel staff are often as ignorant as employees on this subject, which suggests that violations of a basic U.S. labor law are rampant. Nowadays, with enforcement of the nondiscrimination laws fading rapidly, it is important for women to familiarize themselves with older, well-established employment laws that apply equally to men and women. The granddaddy of these is the Fair Labor Standards Act of 1938 (as amended to the present), which spells out the occupations classified as exempt and nonexempt.

First, let's dispense with some of your confusions. The F.L.S.A. has nothing to do with a company's organization chart nor with pay scales; it has to do with the duties and responsibilities of individual employees regardless of their titles or whether they are paid on the basis of salary, hourly wage, fee, or piecework. With a few specific exceptions (primarily among state and local government employees), most American workers are automatically classified as either nonexempt or exempt whether they work in a factory, office, school, or home; for the government, a profit or nonprofit organization; as full-time or part-time employees.

Basically, this act establishes minimum wage, overtime pay, equal pay, record keeping and child labor standards *unless a specific exemption applies.* In other words, most employers, large and small, are subject to the standards that mandate payment of the minimum wage and overtime payment at one-and-a-half times the employee's base rate for any work time beyond 40 hours in a normal work week. To escape these strictures, employers can claim an "exemption" for certain employees in various jobs.

The primary effect of an exempt claim is that it eliminates the need to pay for overtime. As long as a worker is nonexempt, the employer must pay overtime (in dollars, by the way, not in compensatory time off) whenever a worker stays late—even voluntarily—to work on employer business or takes work home. It is never illegal to work overtime; it is only illegal for an employer to fail to pay for it. Exempt employees, on the other hand, can work ten or twelve hours a day, come in weekends or on vacation, take work home regularly, and not get paid one cent more than their regular salary. As you can see, exempt categories can be very beneficial to employers if they can get eager, ambitious employees to work extra hours for nothing. Many women fall for this sophisticated form of exploitation because they erroneously believe that an exempt category is superior to a nonexempt one. That's not necessarily so; fantastically well-paid engineers are commonly nonexempts. Many times women put themselves into low pay brackets from which they can never recover by failing to notice that many exempt jobs can be just as dead-end as nonexempt jobs.

Legally, there are four categories of exempt jobs: (1) bona fide "executives," (2) bona fide "administrative" employees, (3) bona fide "professionals," and (4) outside sales people. Fortunately, the rules—familiarly known as the 541 Regulations—rigidly define each of these four categories and *all* the tests must be met before an employee can be called "exempt." Whether employees are exempt depends on their job duties and responsibilities and the salary paid. The salary requirement for exemption is so low by today's inflated standard ($250 a week or $13,000 a year) that it's not unusual for nonexempts to earn more than that. But meeting this salary minimum does not change the other requirements; those that spell out what the employee must actually *do* on the job to qualify for the exemption. Job titles, incidentally, are irrelevant; what counts are the tasks and responsibilities demanded of the employee.

For instance, an "executive" must have responsibility for the management of the enterprise (or a substantive department or subdivision); regularly direct the work of at least two or more other employees; and have power to hire and fire, evaluate performance, discipline, set pay rates, distribute work, and otherwise exercise discretionary judgment. Only a minimal percentage of an executive's time can be spent on "nonexempt" tasks such as performing production work, especially the same kind of work as done by the employees supervised. A "working supervisor" who continues to do the same work as subordinates may well be illegally classified if called exempt. If she earns less than $13,000, her time spent on routine work cannot exceed twenty percent, for instance.

The "administrative" exemption is one where many women get

caught. Just changing an employee's title to "administrative assistant" does not make her exempt. She must spend the majority of her time and effort on work where she customarily and regularly exercises "discretion and independent judgment." That phrase is the key to any exempt claim. Such work involves setting prices, negotiating contracts, holding meetings, conducting performance appraisals—not merely passing instructions or writing memos. Legitimate administrative jobs include staff specialists, such as those in tax, insurance, and market research, as well as credit managers, purchasing agents, buyers, personnel directors, and executive secretaries who carry on the work of absent executives in an independent fashion (that is, with authority to make important decisions on their own initiative).

Now we get to your category—"professionals." Prima facie evidence of a professional is the appropriate academic degree, but, in addition, such an employee must do work that is predominantly intellectual and varied and requires consistent exercise of discretion and judgment as distinguished from routine, mechanical, or technical duties. To quote from paragraph 541:

Many accountants are exempt as professional employees . . . however, exemption of accountants, as in the case of other occupational groups, must be determined on the basis of the individual employee's duties and the other criteria in the regulations. Accounting clerks, junior accountants, and other accountants normally perform a great deal of routine work . . . where these facts are found such accountants are not exempt.

Since you didn't describe your job duties, I assume you are a nonexempt employee. As such, you are entitled to overtime pay; do not "donate" any extra time to your job or you will put your company in violation of the Fair Labor Standards Act. If the opposite is true and you've been called exempt and are expected to work overtime without pay, you have a ready solution. Look in the phone book under U.S. Government and get the phone number of the local office of the Wage and Hour Division of the Department of Labor. Simply call up and explain your situation to them and find out if you're being paid fairly or classified correctly. This division treats all calls as confidential and will even institute anonymous investigations if it suspects that a company is fudging on compliance with exempt/nonexempt regulations. Even if you have no complaint, you should call and request two booklets: the *Handy Reference Guide to the Fair Labor Standards Act* and *Regulations, 541: Determining Executive, Administrative, Professional, and Outside Sales Exemptions.*

This is a complex law, and I've only hinted at some of its broad ramifications for women's jobs, job duties, and job titles. But all working women should be alerted that the F.L.S.A. has an equal pay provision that prohibits a wage differential between men and women doing equal—not identical—work under similar working conditions. The equal pay provisions apply to both nonexempt and exempt positions. This law and the Wage and Hour Division are two friends ambitious women should assiduously cultivate.

Attempting to translate legal and regulatory governmentese into simple terminology that accurately purveys the intent and interpretation of the law is not a task to approach lightly. Labor law (including nondiscrimination statutes) is especially abstruse because it is designed (and continually amended) to achieve the humanly impossible: Apply to every single type of job in every occupation that exists (or may exist), in every city or hamlet in the United States, in anticipation of every kind of situation that might occur—except those specifically excluded.

To tamper with the necessarily convoluted language of employment laws is fraught with danger. Any distortion, however unwitting, can seriously mislead employees about their job rights and leave them open to disavowal or manipulation by management representatives. Knowing this, I checked my conclusions with appropriate legal, governmental and compensation authorities; I wanted to be ready for some of the nitpicking criticisms I expected. In fact, I got only one unsolicited letter. This is it.

*Dear Ms. Harragan:*

*I read your article with great interest and pleasure. It is a source of satisfaction to me to know that I, in some way, contributed. Let me say that your answer successfully captured the content and flavor* of the 541 Regulations, summarizing and highlighting them in an accurate and easy-to-understand manner.

Congratulations on a job well done.

Raymond G. Cordelli
Assistant Regional Administrator
Wage Hour Division
Employment Standards Administration
U.S. Department of Labor (New York)


# WHAT'S A "SECRETARY"?

*Dear Betty Harragan:*

I have been a professional secretary for ten years and like it very much. There are many like me. My current job as private secretary to the president of a small financial institution involves a lot of agony, sweat and toil (by both me and my boss) but is fascinating and has given me a business education. (My secret dream is to someday start a company like this myself.)

Nevertheless my job is riddled with problems. One is the location of my desk, which is situated to block access to my boss but leaves me completely exposed. I can't get my work done because of constant interruptions from people who approach me as if I'm a receptionist or information bureau. Another is salary. When I started, I negotiated a sum of $1,150 a month with the understanding that I'd be considered for a substantial raise after six months. Now I see that "consider" is a very weak word; I can be "considered" indefinitely, just to keep me on the hook. I've been thinking of different titles: Office manager? No. Administrative assistant? No. What, then? Some of my colleagues have tried to rise above the secretarial level this way only to be told they don't have enough education or the right experience for promotion. But what about those like me who want to be secretaries?

I hear about seminars on career development but I have not found any company, no matter how many billions of dollars in sales it makes, that will pay up to $595 for a secretary to attend. (That's *more than most of us make in a month!) How do I go about tapping into these valuable information centers? Is there anything I can do about my problems?*

*Committed*

Dear Committed:

Believe me, I give more thought to the secretarial job than to any other single occupation. I consider the role of the secretary in today's business world to be a pivot, or fulcrum, around which the fate of female professional and managerial aspirants rotates; no job more accurately reflects the *real* attitude of management toward any and all women employees. The plight of the secretary should be everyone's concern.

As things now stand, experienced, dedicated secretaries are the most undervalued, underpaid, unappreciated and unclassified workers in the American labor economy. The fact that almost ninety-nine percent of them are women is very significant. As you no doubt know, the job doesn't even *exist!* There is no box on the organization chart for "secretary." There is no career track; there is no job description, and consequently there is no salary scale. How can compensation experts attach a salary scale to a nonexistent job? They can't, so they don't. Secretaries are simply lumped into an amorphous white-collar puddle labeled "unskilled workers" commonly identified as clericals or, more trenchantly, "women office workers."

It's for this reason that I continually warn all ambitious women who do *not* want to be secretaries never to accept any job with that title. It's the supreme dead end, and, worse yet, the experience gained in that position will not be counted in their job history if and when they escape to nontraditional ranks, i.e., to any job not labeled "clerical."

You are correct, however, in pointing out that the situation of career secretaries like yourself has too long been ignored. The first move that you—and all other private secretaries—must make is to force your bosses to "see" that you perform an explicit job. For instance, you mention that your desk placement interferes with accomplishing "my work." Clearly, it has not occurred to your boss that you have any independent duties. You are being treated as nothing more than a charming, helpful, smiling receptionist. I'm not suggesting your boss consciously believes that or deliberately set it up that way; most likely he never thought about it at all! It's up to you to explain it to him, to tell him that he must make the decision about your priorities—either you are a public relations front or you perform the substantive tasks he expects from you.

Don't, whatever you do, try to handle both jobs simultaneously and drive yourself into an agonized sweat to get "your" work done despite the interruptions. Very practically, you might suggest he install a ceiling-to-floor glass panel outside your desk to effectively block unwarranted intrusions. If space allows, you can ask for a private office, or perhaps a suite for the two of you. I take it your relationship with your boss is congenial (as it should be), so you may have no trouble making him "see" the job you do.

Some executives, though, will slough off such a request, saying, "Do the best you can. I'm sure it's not that disturbing." In such an event you'll have to take the initiative for the priority decision. Since it's not wise to antagonize customers, employees or the public, your priority is: Be pleasant to all interrupters. Graciously respond to these people *but* keep an accurate, split-second, *written* record of every distraction episode, every day. As your own work suffers, let the tasks accumulate, uncompleted. When your boss asks for results (or you deem it politic to warn about the mounting lapses), produce your distraction time-sheets and show him exactly where he has unwittingly allocated your time. Ask again if that's what he prefers you to do—or does he want to solve the privacy problem as you recommended?

Historically, secretaries have allowed themselves to be put down, partly because they don't place a solid business value on their own contributions and partly because they cling to outmoded ideas of what a wage-paying job is. Happily, that situation has taken a decided turn for the better. You may feel reassured to hear that you are not alone in taking a realistic stand to improve your own job satisfaction. Answers to a survey in the March 26, 1981, issue of *Personal Report for the Professional Secretary*, published by the Research Institute of America, were compared to those from a similar survey conducted in 1972. The difference in attitudes was striking. Nine years earlier secretaries came across as people whose working lives centered on their boss and his concerns. Nowadays, nearly half place their own welfare first. Incidentally, a whopping two-thirds said women supervisors can be just as effective as men. Most dramatically, when asked about salary, ninety percent of the respondents indicated anger because their salaries do not reflect the seriousness and responsibility the job entails. In 1972 salary was such a nonissue that the topic wasn't even raised!

Despite their well-documented job problems, forty percent of the women surveyed said they would choose the same profession all over again. Projected on a national scale, that figure suggests that some two million working secretaries today feel as you do—they like their jobs, believe they are integral to the smooth functioning of their organizations, and, in the majority, are willing to fight for appropriate rights and rewards. This is a stunning reversal of the old stereotype of the docile, fuddy-duddy secretary. You are in good company.

Even more exciting is the sudden emergence of a dynamic leadership cadre. To my great surprise, the staid, conservative, forty-year-old National Secretaries Association (newly named Professional Secretaries International) has managed a complete turn-around. In launching an unprecedented Secretary Speakout in San Francisco in March 1981, then-president Nancy DeMars said, "Everybody has been speaking for the secretary, except the professional career secretary. It is time we identify ourselves, speak to our concerns, take positive positions and develop a consensus on how to address our manifest problems." The consensus statement started off: "APPRECIATION DOES NOT REPLACE COMPENSA-TION."

Important as these developments are, the reality remains that each individual must negotiate her own raises. As you've already discovered, this takes action, not passive "understandings" or vague hopes to be "considered." To get a deserved raise you have to ask for a specific number of dollars as of a specified date. Incidentally, forget about fancy titles; you don't want them anyway. You want to be fairly compensated for the job you handle in a partnership alliance with your boss.

First, find out (or estimate) how much your boss makes. That will give you the best clue as to local industry norms, since the dollar value of the executive function in which you participate has already been established. Don't pay any attention to clerical salary ranges. A private secretary is more like a quasi-management employee, so I strongly suggest you take a tip from management and discuss salary figures in annual, not monthly or weekly, amounts. You are making $13,800; your executive partner is making— $40,000, $50,000, $70,000, more? If he is making $70,000, you'd have a $56,000 difference in your salaries or, put another way, he'd be making 500 percent more than you. Do his contribution, experience, job history, age, responsibility warrant so huge a spread? You might easily be justified in asking that your salary be doubled.

Of course, that leads straight to the key consideration: How indispensable are you to this boss? Would his productivity be severely impaired without your collaboration? How long would it take to hire and train a replacement for you? How much would it cost the company if you left? Not only in replacement costs but in lowered efficiency or effective operation—or actual revenue growth—in the interim?

Then, here's your trump card. How many experienced, dedicated professional secretaries are out there clamoring for a high-pressure job that pays roughly $8,000 a year in inflation-adjusted dollars? (For example, between January 1975 and March 1981 the inflation rate went *up* 69.37 percent.) Will they find *anybody* with your qualifications, much less someone who will take as little as you earn now?

The answer is "No."

Surely you've heard about the secretarial shortage? Management certainly has, but they are counting on "dumb" secretaries being unable to figure out that a shortage of oil, sugar, chocolate or anything else causes prices for that commodity to skyrocket. Why hasn't that basic economic law of supply and demand worked for secretaries?

It hasn't worked because secretaries aren't aware of it, or don't use it. I can't tell you how much of a raise to ask for because every secretary's situation is different; you have to figure it out for yourself based on an analysis of what your job is worth in your particular partnership, using questions such as those I've posed.

But I can tell you one thing: If you—and all other professional secretaries—genuinely believe (as I do) that your job contributions are essential to a healthy American business society, you will *stop* selling your brains, ability and hard-earned expertise for poverty-level wages. Right now.

No doubt about it, secretaries are dynamite. The very word touches off explosions large and small from myriad directions. Certainly this column prompted a stream of reactions from secretaries, ex-secretaries, clericals, professionals, employer representatives (personnel managers), compensation consultants, career developers, employment agencies and newsletter publishers. Any secretary who feels her job is looked upon as unimportant can rest assured that is not the case; keeping secretaries in their place is a big, profitable business across the entire employment spectrum.

We all have a million miles to go before this key occupation can be seen with clarity. The secretarial function is so densely woven into the fabric of organizations that attempts to isolate it as an independent warp-or-woof strand threaten the familiar texture of American industry. Big employers, therefore, sense the imminent danger to their structural foundations if a vital component of the underlying support staff insists on explicit job descriptions and comparable pay schedules. Some companies fight tooth and nail to maintain the status quo, but others try to neutralize this potential time-bomb with superficial changes to obfuscate the picture; the proliferation of newly coined job titles intended to mask secretarial duties is a popular technique. For reasons unbeknownst to me, the quickest to be fooled by cosmetic changes are some female personnel managers. Predictably then, they were among the first to get into the ensuing dialogue.

*Dear Betty Harragan:*

*How can you be so unrealistic about the professional secretary? As a secretary who started at the bottom and worked her way up, I am now manager of two departments: personnel and office services. I see to it that we have up-to-date job descriptions, and there certainly is a place on the organization chart—directly under the executive, as a matter of fact—for the secretary. As far as the salary scale, we*

*have that, too. We use the Hay job evaluation system, and secre-*
*taries are valued higher than many of the "professional" clerical*
*positions in the office such as senior accounting clerk, senior data*
*processing coordinators, senior customer service assistants and senior*
*personnel assistants.*

*I'm sure there are many companies guilty of these accusations but*
*there are also many that are concerned about secretarial positions,*
*and have put forth tremendous efforts to correct this problem. As a*
*personnel manager, I suggest that secretaries who feel they are in a*
*hopeless position bring their discontent to the attention of their supe-*
*riors—and don't go in with complaints, go in with solutions.*

*Office Personnel Manager*

Dear Manager:

I know some companies are trying to clean out the snake pit of
clerical devaluation, but most of the efforts perpetuate the gross
inequities that exist. Granted, the problems are enormous but they
will never be solved if personnel managers don't come down from
Cloud Nine. For instance, you say that secretaries have a spot on
your organization chart directly under the executive. If so, that
indicates that each is in line for promotion to the boss's job and it
would further mandate that the secretary's salary be next highest to
the executive's, above all other subordinates in the department. I
suppose this is possible but I'd be astounded if it were true. In fact,
it sounds like you've continued the age-old practice of indicating
"secretary" in the executive box to show that position is entitled to a
personal aide.

As for your job descriptions for secretaries, how accurate are
they? Do they actually delineate the *individualized* duties and specific job content of each secretarial position? To my knowledge, the
Hay System does not do this, so if you're relying on it you haven't
progressed far. Since you are depending on technical job evaluation, are you using the *same* factors and weighting scale for secretarial jobs as for all others in the managerial, technical and
professional categories? If you have not included *all* employees
equally in your job analyses, then you have simply formalized traditional systems based on sex-segregated job values—one set for
predominantly men's jobs, a different set for predominantly

women's jobs. It's hardly innovative to pay secretaries more than clericals; executive secretaries have always been the elite of the clerical corps.

What intrigues me is your unique euphemism for meaningless titles (assistant, coordinator, etc.); you refer to them as "professional" clericals. There is no such thing. It connotes an illegal category called "exempt-nonexempts." This could signify a violation of the Fair Labor Standards Act (very serious), or else it is an attempt to substitute phony titles in lieu of honest point-factor job evaluations and pay scales.

*Dear Betty Harragan:*

*I take offense at women putting down other women and other positions, especially those on the first rungs of the corporate ladder. The receptionist at our bank is considered one of the most important professional staff members in our organization. She is usually the first employee with whom customers come in contact either by phone or in person and from whom they get their first impressions of our entire corporation. Her professional demeanor is essential; she is an invaluable asset to management.*

*The receptionist of any organization reflects its initial image. Thus, a description of this position as being "nothing more than a charming, helpful, smiling receptionist" is degrading to the entire clerical profession. Should clerical positions always be lumped as a negative force of management? The narrow definition of clericals as people who answer the phone, type and file does not fit any more. This profession deserves as much credit as the other vital ones within a successful organization.*

*Director of Personnel*

Dear P.D.:

I'm the first to agree that a good receptionist is an invaluable asset to management and that the function she performs is necessary and useful. But in your description of the job I fail to find requirements that go beyond being "charming, helpful, smiling" (unless your bank chooses to project a contrary image, which is implausible). I'd like to applaud your efforts to upgrade and glamorize this position, except that such attempts are inherently dishonest.

You identify her as a "professional staff member," but that is not so. Her job is furthest away from being "professional," as are the other clerical positions, which you describe as "this profession." As a personnel professional yourself, you have an obligation to become better informed about proper job nomenclature and to acquire rudimentary knowledge of the wage and hour laws. (See pages 78-83 for the difference between clerical and professional positions.) You can easily judge how much value management places on this "invaluable asset" by consulting the salary records. Money is the infallible measuring rod used by managements to establish the ranking of all employees, from top to bottom. I think you'll find the receptionist job is located near the bottom of that financial ladder.

The responsibility of the personnel department is to locate an individual who will like that job, enjoy the public contacts, be satisfied with the salary, and convey the desired image of the corporation; to portray the job as something other than it is insults the employee's intelligence.

Despite the insensitivity of too many personnel departments, secretaries themselves are not easily deluded anymore. A surprising number expressed sorrow that managements around the country are too obtuse to recognize the contributions of women who could be the company's most loyal, dedicated, productive workers, but the mood in the trenches is overwhelmingly melancholy as the problems persist.

*Dear Betty Harragan:*

*I've been employed in the secretarial field for seventeen years. I started at the bottom and worked my way up to an office manager position. I have the responsibility but have never reaped the rewards that should go along with the title. For the past seven years I was employed by a giant corporation; I recently resigned to take a job in a smaller but still very large company. My starting salary at my new job is higher than my salary after seven years with the giant. This should tell us all something about salary scales. I know some of the inequities are being worked on, but we still have a long, long way to go.*

*Ohio*

Dear Ohio:

What this tells us about salaries is that they *are* negotiable, even among similar companies in the same city. It also tells us that loyalty or passive hope for fair treatment is not a successful strategy; job hopping is much better.

*Dear Betty Harragan:*

*Having read about the secretarial shortage, I can only assume that the main problem lies in defining "secretary." I have been a secretary for ten years, since attending a secretarial college in San Francisco. I have not used my shorthand but I have used my skills in business correspondence, grammar, spelling, administrative office procedures, basic accounting and information retrieval. In interviews, however, the only skill defined or demanded has been typing. If the ability to type is the only measurable job criterion, how can the value of a secretary be determined? After all, anyone without a severe mental or physical impairment can be trained to type. Until executives can determine a professional definition of their secretarial requirements, secretaries cannot make the demands on prospective employers that you recommend.*

*California*

Dear California:

Oh yes, you can. (But you might have to take an assertiveness course to get over the submissive attitudes you apparently absorbed from secretarial school; they are as obsolete as your shorthand seems to be.) The current supply-and-demand ratio strongly favors experienced secretaries, but you cannot wait for management to come up with a definition of the job. Each individual secretary must take the initiative in defining her own skills and putting a price on them. Fend off the typing tests as irrelevant until you're offered a job; instead, interview the prospective boss about the functions expected of you. Ask how much use they have for information retrieval, independent correspondence, accounting, administrative responsibility—whatever you prefer to do. With the widespread shortage, good secretaries should no more take typist's jobs than engineers take drafting jobs. Keep looking until you find an employer who accepts *your* definition of a career secretarial position and is willing to pay the salary you decide your experience is worth. It's hard to remember that ten years ago Executive Secretary was the ultimate job for women in a blatantly discriminatory workforce. By and large, secretaries were a quiescent group happy to get a rose on their desk once a year as a sign the boss loved them. There were no job descriptions then, either, but there was an informal understanding among clerical employees that if they worked hard all their lives, didn't complain, and improved their skills and tenure, they might someday achieve the coveted private secretary position.

Then the gates were opened through equal employment (E.E.O.) and affirmative action laws and women could apply for, aspire to, and seek promotion to hundreds of positions that had previously been closed to them. By the thousands, ambitious women bounded out of the secretarial jail house while loads of entering women disdained the clerical jobs that were limited to training secretaries. At the same time, holdover secretaries—those who like that kind of work and now want the job reclassified as a professional occupation specialty—began to examine the day-by-day tasks they performed. They tried to jettison the outmoded housework-handmaiden-office-wife activities that were frequently attached and concentrate on the indispensable business requirements.

As of now, this occupation is a mess. It is in the process of transition. The situation is further confused by the rapid introduction of computerized automation systems that are creating their own mess. Office work will be altered considerably in coming years, but I predict that electronic information systems will have less deleterious impact on the professional secretary job than on the executives and managers. The transformation of the secretarial job will come about as dedicated secretaries like you keep defining the parameters of the job to your employers, not vice versa.

*Dear Betty Harragan:*

*I'm getting sick and tired of companies advertising for a secretary and misleading the applicant with job titles. What does a secretary mean to a company today? After a continuous record of working as a secretary for ten years, I've recently gone through agonizing experiences with three major companies.*

*The first, with a computer manufacturer, involved no work what-
soever. When I asked the boss for work he said he had none—so I sat
at my desk in this so-called secretarial position for six weeks before I
quit in disgust. Job Number Two turned out to be another fiasco
with no work but with a wise-cracking, smart-alecky boss. Job Number Three was with a large corporate headquarters and, although
titled secretary, the job was dictaphone-typist—no phone, no communication with the boss, no connection to the rest of the office
staff. What's the matter with these personnel experts who misrepre-
sent jobs? Dictaphone-typist is a far cry from secretary. I can run a
whole office in the absence of a boss, but they believe anyone who
sits at a desk is a secretary. This was once a beautiful profession but
now we women are treated like we have no brains whatsoever.*

*New Jersey*

Dear Jersey:

I think you are running into a fact-of-life about the role of secretary that you've never considered or prefer to avoid: One of the
primary duties of a private secretary is to serve as a human status
symbol for a senior executive. If you find that hard to believe (as
many secretaries do), just analyze your recent experiences.

You stumbled across not one, but two, major corporations that
were obviously advertising for and hiring a secretary when—as you
subsequently discovered—there was literally no work to do. Yet
these two companies were willing to pay you a salary to fill a vacancy that *had* to be filled. Why? Two completely separate bosses
told you they had no substantive work to pass on to you but they
just wanted you to sit there (and look pretty?) or, in one case, just
kid around. Evidently, the present economic doldrums have severely curtailed their own workloads but it is imperative that each
one maintains his own status and clout within his organization. To
do so, he has to have "a secretary" sitting at the proper desk;
whether you had any productive work function was immaterial—
you were being paid to be a status symbol.

One of the obvious inequities *within* the secretarial occupation is
that some highly paid senior secretaries do much less work than
secretaries to lower- or middle-management executives—who get
paid much less. That's because secretaries' salaries are calculated

according to the hierarchical ranking of the boss, not on the productivity, merit, or ability of the secretary. Wage and salary experts (including outside compensation consultants) are responsible for perpetuating this disgraceful state of affairs. That's why supposedly fair job evaluation systems are never fair to secretaries. Nobody dares challenge the subterranean function of the secretary—her role as status symbol.

I can give you further proof, if proof is necessary. This powerful game ploy is commonly used to demean or "demote" female executives who have reached senior executive levels. Frequently, a woman will be promoted to a relatively high position with the same rank and title as a previous male incumbent—except that she won't get the private secretary that customarily went with the job. In the last year or so I've heard reports of high-level women executives who suddenly "lost their secretary." The move was taken under the guise of budget cuts, reducing overhead, or hiring freezes, but everybody in the company knew the executive had lost clout and, indeed, that her job might be in jeopardy because she wasn't able to fend off this public slap in the face.

Under tight economic constraints, jobs tend to boil down to their indispensable elements; as you found out, the single function of a secretary that cannot be eliminated is her status significance. By contrast, you also found out what the title "secretary" means when stripped of that item—it means any routine clerical job that requires typing. These are cruel realizations for people who take pride in their skills and performance, but everyone who is committed to redefining the job of secretary must take these clandestine factors into account.

Incidentally, if you are qualified to run an office when the boss is away, yet ended up with these job offers, you must be putting a very low price tag on your skills and experience.

*Dear Betty Harragan:*

*I worked as secretary to a vice-president of a national company. I enjoyed my work and learned a great deal from being exposed to upper-management decisions and responsibilities. However, the knowledge I attained was never rewarded or recognized. Because of this I tried to break out of the secretary mold and advance in an-*

*other area of the company. It was impossible; my boss wanted to keep me as a secretary and kept promising promotions that never materialized even though two possibilities occurred. This continued for a couple of years until I realized the game he was playing. I made an agonizing decision to quit and return to school to complete a degree in finance and accounting. When I gave notice, my boss told me I was too old to return to school because I'd be twenty-six by the time I graduated and would never find a job in the accounting field.*

*I'll be graduating soon and my aim is to become a C.P.A. I value the lessons I learned as a secretary although some hurt me deeply. It's sad that management does not realize the true value of the professional secretary.*

*Colorado*

Dear Colorado:

Good for you for quitting. When an allegedly intelligent executive says twenty-six is too old to start a credentialed career, he's exposing his own stupidity or treating you like an unmitigated idiot. He's good riddance.

Your experience illustrates why it does so little good to raise the consciousness of "management." Under the historic (and continuing) set-up, private secretaries don't benefit much from company policies because their work world is a tiny enclave dominated almost exclusively by the executive they are assigned to. It is almost impossible, as you discovered, to break this parasitic bond. Although a national corporation lost a devoted, ambitious employee in you, that was less important than giving that selfish creep complete control over your future. You had no recourse but to quit. As long as secretaries remain structured into the hierarchy as appendages to executives, instead of being judged and paid for their own contributions, abandonment of the occupation is the ambitious young woman's most promising alternative.

*Dear Betty Harragan:*

*I wound up in a secretarial position in government because I needed a summer job during college. A family friend (male person-*

*nel officer) suggested I take the civil service clerical exam. My typing was so lousy I failed three times before passing to get a clerk-typist job. Financial difficulties forced me to continue working full time and attending school part time at night. It took years to get my degree in Public Administration. I still get the lame excuses I got before my degree—that I don't have the exact qualifications, education, experience, training, etc., that will allow me to shift into government professional fields.*

*If I had known when I first accepted a clerk-typist position that I would wind up in a dead-end job as a secretary, there is no way I would have accepted. I hate the field! There is no upward mobility, promotion is limited, and women who are secretaries are seen as "nobodies." I've expanded my present position to the point where I train psychologists, program analysts and other professionals, but when I approach my boss about a title change he goes through the motions of having me rewrite job descriptions and says he passes the requests through channels. The last time I pressured him, the order came back that the "slot" is to remain "secretarial." I did locate a management analyst position I was offered in another agency but then the Reagan administration ceilings came down and that was the end of that.*

*My experience shows how people end up in secretarial positions for lack of information. I've found over the years that one must persistently seek accurate information; it does not come to you.*

*Maryland*

Dear Maryland:

You've demonstrated why I consistently warn women who do *not* want to be lifetime secretaries to stay far away from the field, even for summer employment. It is a trap that lures unwary young women who need a job, but for the ambitious it invariably becomes an albatross around your neck because "once a secretary, always a secretary" seems to be imprinted across the eyeballs of all employers and employment agents. That wouldn't be bad except that the perception—the stereotype—of secretaries is universally derogatory. The professional secretaries association understands that "image" is one of the big obstacles to upgrading the occupation and gives it high priority among the many problems that need addressing. As long as you're still a secretary, you may be interested in helping:

Professional Secretaries International
2440 Pershing Road
Crown Center G10
Kansas City, MO 64108
(816) 477-5755

P.S.I., founded as the National Secretaries Association in 1942, has hundreds of local chapters all over the United States and Canada. It publishes an excellent monthly magazine, *The Secretary*, which includes many business articles that are equally relevant to nonsecretarial professionals.

*Dear Betty Harragan:*

*I am part of the one percent, a male secretary. I've been in the clerical field for eight years, a professional secretary for one. I'm employed by a large financial institution and my boss is a woman.*

*I'm seated at one end of the floor and my boss's office is at the other end. Needless to say, my legs get a lot of exercise but otherwise this placement creates no problem. Interruptions are part of the job. Everyone expects the secretary to know where the boss is at all times, no matter what. People also expect the secretary to know as much as the boss does about the functions of the company. As far as public relations, the secretary gives the first impression of the boss and the company. This is an extremely important aspect of the job: All telephone calls and visitors must be treated in a congenial, respectful manner and the secretary must exercise an acquired talent, diplomacy, and keep smiling.*

*The titles "office manager" and "administrative assistant" are nothing more than euphemisms for the word secretary. For too long secretaries have been regarded as brainless nonentities; these and similar titles suggest that the person is intelligent and bright (although many times that person is not). I am a valued employee, I am not underpaid, and am appreciated on both a personal and employment level. Many secretarial complaints are not problems at all, simply parts of the job—routine, as it were.*

*Baltimore*

Dear Baltimore:
Smart woman, your boss.

## WHERE WOMEN COLLIDE

*Dear Betty Harragan:*
*I'm assistant to a respected vice-president of a large travel agency and I want to stay here because I think there is room for me to grow. When I was hired a year ago, my boss assured me I could move to a more challenging position within the company when one opens up. My problem began two months ago when he told me I would also be handling the correspondence of a new member of our department—a woman sales manager whom few of the fifty women in our division can tolerate. She constantly mentions that she's the first woman in our business, as if the rest of us don't count! She puts on an un-failingly cheerful, sugary sweet act toward everyone. I admit she is unbelievably good at her job and is always nice to me and very complimentary about my work. How can I handle a woman whose actions are so condescending she offends me and most of the other women? What can I do besides grit my teeth and try to do the work if I want the job? This situation is really upsetting me.*

*Unhappy*

Dear Unhappy:
You have neatly described one facet of what I consider the most dangerous predicament facing ambitious women in the 1980s: the inevitable collision of women employees who now function at vary-ing levels in the organization hierarchy. How you handle this rela-tionship to a senior woman may have more influence on your job prospects than all the technical know-how you can acquire in a lifetime.

Your problem is by no means as simple as it looks on paper. You sense this instinctively, because you seem hard put to find something wrong with your boss beyond the general observation that everyone hates her. Since the resentment apparently surfaced almost before she walked in the door, she can hardly be the generator of the difficulty. As a matter of fact, from your description, she sounds like an ideal boss and a charming workday colleague—cheerful, complimentary, nice, appreciative, capable.

If she were a man in that same job, how would those qualities strike you? Judging from the fair, even tone of your letter, I suspect you'd say "wonderful," or "too good to be true." And you'd be right. People of high professional caliber, with sunny dispositions (in what is undeniably a high-pressure industry), are about as common as hen's teeth. Indeed, she seems to prove the popular adage that women have to be twice (or ten times) as good as men to get substantial jobs. Why, then, does this constellation of stellar qualities offend you when the person possessing them happens to be female? I wonder if that could be what is upsetting you; even to yourself, your reaction doesn't make sense.

It's little wonder that you can't fathom the reason for your underlying hostility. Its source lies buried deep in a tangled skein composed of business reality, cultural conditioning, sexism, psychology, feminine taboos, changing economic conditions. Let's take one visible loose end—business reality—and see where it leads.

Job classification *exists* as a real-life factor in the employment world. No amount of obfuscation by title or euphemism, such as "assistant to" or "take the correspondence of," disguises the reality that your job is classified as "secretary," and that locates it in the huge nonexempt job category known as "clerical." Presumably, your women co-workers are similarly classified even though they have assorted titles or duties. You all know full well what the new executive means when she admits she is the "first woman" in that business. She means she is the first female in a managerial job category with an upward track, or, perhaps, the first woman to break through the discriminatory clerical barrier and be classified in the professional, exempt category. That's a plain fact, as indisputable as her eye color, height—or gender.

There's nothing condescending about publicizing this fact. She *should* keep management aware that it's unconscionable in the 1980s that she is the only female executive in a company loaded with lower-level ambitious women. Also, she might *have* to hammer this point repeatedly just to get the respect due her position and not to be treated as "one of the girls in the clerical ranks" (which is where your company obviously believes women "belong").

Those of you located on the clerical level, which may be several ranks below her grade, are displaying a business naiveté that will keep you at that level forever because your hostile attitude alerts management that you refuse to accept the job-ranking system (or chain-of-command) that is indispensable to organizational structure. You take a lone woman's upgrading as an insult to yourselves, i.e., "as if the rest of us don't count." I hate to puncture your daydream, but that's true; you don't. Only it isn't her fault, it's management's. Clerical workers are customarily looked upon as part of overhead, not as essential contributors to money-making operations. (Now! If you all want to challenge *that* business reality, you'll have a cause worthy of your combined rage.)

You say you have ambitions to progress beyond the clerical ranks yourself. If successful, how do you plan to function at a higher level? Exactly as you do at the clerical level, denying that job grade means anything? Since you are offended by sugary sweetness, does that mean you would behave in an opposite manner—mean, unpleasant, critical, destructive, disparaging? Even more important, where will you, as a future executive, get your support staff, since the clerical-level employees in your division seem determined not to "tolerate" even a superbly qualified female executive?

I notice that the first woman manager was severely undercut from the outset by her male superior (the same vice-president you are depending on). Obviously, he did not think a sales manager (female) was important enough to have a full-time secretary although her job responsibilities must be overwhelming. Instead, she is expected to make do with any odd moments his full-time assistant (you) can spare for her correspondence. Actually, that is an insult to both you and her. (I can safely predict your salary didn't double when you were assigned to do two full-time secretarial jobs.)

If you are really serious about your own career, you're in a great position to take a calculated risk. Go to the male vice-president and explain that the sales manager needs a full-time secretary of her own. Then suggest that he hire a new secretary to work for him because you will transfer to the woman sales manager. After all, she needs an experienced assistant like you desperately; and you need her to be successful because any chances you have in that company will depend on the outcome of the management's "gamble" on its first token woman.

Besides, you can learn a lot from her about women's job problems at higher levels, while all you'll learn from the male v.p. is that you are indispensable—so the dangling carrot of a "more challenging position" is forever elusive.

# CHAPTER FIVE

# Promotion Predicaments

## FEAR OF PROMOTION

*Dear Betty Harragan:*
*I work in the product development department of a major organization. I've been here five years and have been steadily promoted to take on more and more responsibility. My boss and I established a very good working relationship, and a year ago he told me he planned to retire in five years and would recommend that I succeed him as head of this division. I thought that five years would give me enough time to grow into the job. I've had some opportunity to work with his boss, the director of the department, and found the experience stimulating and challenging, so I'm sure I could report directly to him in a successful manner.*

*But a terrible thing has happened. My boss had a heart attack and died. Now the director has turned to me and asked me to head the operation. I am very concerned. I worry that I may not be able to meet the challenge called for in the new role. I am bright and well-organized but not the intellectual giant my boss was. I have strengths he lacked, but intellectually he outdistanced me and others. I don't feel quite ready for the manager role. In four years I think I could do the job and feel competent, but right now is a bit*

*too soon. There is so much I have to learn in the field. I feel too*
*young and inexperienced (I'm thirty-five). Do you think I should*
*voice these doubts to the director?*

*Conflicted*

Dear Conflicted:

I shudder to think of the number of readers who would give
anything to be in your shoes, to be offered a managerial position
years before they expected it. On the other hand, I know several
women who were promoted too far, too fast, and after a stressful
few years, eventually failed at the jobs. Lady Luck comes dressed in
a variety of garbs.

Fortunately, you've had ample time to observe and analyze the
requirements of the position and to assess your strengths and weaknesses in meeting those responsibilities. Moreover, you've looked
ahead to the crucial determinant—the change in the reporting relationship—and concluded that you could work successfully in direct
contact with the department head who would be your new boss. In
fact, you admit that you'd feel stimulated and challenged in that
circumstance, indicating that you respect the director's decisions
and methods of operation. All in all, the prognosis for this promotion seems too good to be true—except for your nagging inner
doubts.

Precisely what strikes you as so negative? Your overpowering fear
of measuring up to standards set by your deceased boss? Obviously
you admired his work tremendously and must be extremely grateful
because he promoted you this far and was grooming you to be his
successor. But your appreciation of his good qualities goes far
beyond the normal. An "intellectual giant" who outdistanced you
and others? He didn't outdistance the director, apparently, nor
those in senior levels of management above that. Rather, he
seemed content to retire from a relatively low mid-management
position. Of course, he could still have been a brilliant man who
gained satisfaction from performing a constant task to perfection (or
maybe he ran into bad luck in his career climb), but this combination hardly justifies the awe with which you regard him.

I think you're misjudging the parameters of the job because
you're evaluating it on the basis of the person who held it—whose

capabilities you also misjudged. You say you have so much to learn before you'll feel ready for the manager role. How do you know what you have to learn? You don't have the job yet; you have no personal experience to help you decide what information is essential to sound performance. I grant you, it's pleasant to work in an environment with intelligent or "intellectual" people who seem boundlessly well informed, but that's usually irrelevant to satisfactory performance of a limited task.

It occurs to me that your idealized boss was irresponsible or egotistical if he led you to believe you had to be the world-champion know-it-all before you could handle his job. Or perhaps you created your own distorted image of what a promotion entails because nobody told you that upward mobility is a process of on-the-job training. Each job is a prerequisite for the next more complex one. You learn as you go. If you had to "know everything" about a field before you take the job designed to teach you, the entire system would be a shambles. As crazy as jobs sometimes seem, the basic concept is not a total absurdity. Those women who fail after moving too fast usually skipped some essential middle steps that prevented their mastering the advanced lessons they became exposed to at higher jobs.

But that's not your case; you've had five years as close associate to the manager. If you're not ready to move ahead now, you never will be. There is no way you can become more competent four years from now except by plunging into the job that will teach you what you need to know. If you try it now and fail to make the grade, be assured you would fail more miserably four years from now. Only I don't think you'll fail. Your boss had faith in your competency; the department head has confidence you can take over the responsibility. Why should you doubt them?

As to your question: Should you discuss your self-doubts with the director? Definitely not! You'll make him question his original evaluation of your abilities and force him to watch your work skeptically, looking for evidence that Daddy's tremulous little girl can't live up to parental expectations. And what, pray tell, is this nonsense that at age thirty-five you feel "young and inexperienced"? To tell the truth, if I hadn't heard this same expression from other women with good educations, good job histories in good firms, I might have misjudged the source of your uncertainty. But anyone who closely observes the contemporary workforce can see how pervasive and debilitating is the American cultural conditioning that stunts female growth at the perpetual level of "girl" and reduces their aspirations to childish proportions.

At your mature age it is very unbecoming to pass yourself off as an adolescent. Try to banish the word "inexperienced" from your mind and vocabulary. Take the job and grow up instantly.

Reaction to this subject came, not from those who shared the feelings of inadequacy, but from those who observed this phenomenon in action. Radio and television talk show hosts whose programs feature listener call-in segments were quick to respond; they reported that they or their guests get many questions that fall into the category of "I'm not sure I'm ready to handle a job I've been offered." Psychologists immediately recognized the problem as one they encounter repeatedly with clients. The prevalence of this amorphous sense of deficiency among otherwise ambitious or independent women seemed to surprise those who heard such confessions. But by far the most confounded are male managers, who sometimes run into a stone wall when they try to promote women with high potential. A Seattle business man spoke for many when he described his frustration.

I have this one woman who's exceptionally capable, bright, personable. She could go far in our company because I see she has the qualifications and personality to handle a substantial job—and we need her. Two or three openings have occurred in the last two years that I asked her to consider. They meant big promotions and I know she could do the job better than the people (men) we hired instead. But she always says she "isn't quite ready," or words to that effect. I like her, we're good friends, I can talk to her frankly, I tell her how much confidence I have in her ability—but I can't convince her. So far I've only succeeded in forcing her to accept an insignificant promotion which is far below her capacity. Sometimes I wonder . . . could it be her husband? Dragging her down at home?

# IMPLICATIONS OF AN "ACTING" TITLE

*Dear Betty Harragan:*

*This hospital has never promoted any woman to an administrative post, so I was stunned when my boss resigned and began pushing for me to succeed him as director of public relations. He admitted encountering some resistance from our department chief but was able to convince the key superiors that I could accomplish a smooth transition when he leaves at the end of the month. Now I'm excited at the prospect, especially since all my interviews and discussions have gone well. We've even discussed my staff and hiring needs to continue a promotional campaign we've just launched. They told me I won't get the same salary as my current boss but that it will be "commensurate with the position." When I tried to bring up dollar figures, the chief said I'd be getting a two-tiered increase rather than a big jump because I'd have the title "acting director" for six months—"in case it doesn't work out." That sounded fair enough at the time, but now I'm having second thoughts. I don't want to quibble over nonsense and jeopardize this opportunity, but why would he spring this "acting" title on me at the last minute? What does it mean?*

*Nervous*

Dear Nervous:

It probably means what you think it means—that this promotion offer is not as straightforward as you want to believe. But you're fortunate that the alarm bell went off in your head before it's too late to reopen negotiations. There's no rush because time is on your side. The closer it gets to the end of the month, the more likely you are to get what you want; they need you to accomplish the transition. What you want is elimination of that word "acting" in the job title. That innocent adjective is far from "quibbling over nonsense." It is the difference between genuine managerial responsibility and being set up as a patsy programmed to fail.

It's hard to believe your superiors would deliberately sabotage you, so start from the assumption that they are inexperienced at dealing with women executives and mean to "protect" you. Whatever their intent, you cannot accept the position if you are merely "acting director" and you will have to get that across to them firmly, pleasantly and gradually. But first you must be very clear in your own mind as to why that title is unacceptable to you for even a day. How you handle this issue will have more impact on your future success than any on-the-job accomplishments. Let's consider what would happen if you let them cajole you into the "acting" title and your new position is announced:

• All your professional colleagues in public relations will know the director job is still open; it hasn't been filled by a qualified person but you have been sweet enough to carry on the work for your employer while they search for a suitable replacement for the man who quit. It's as bad as hanging a sign around your neck that says you are incompetent or unambitious. In government and academia, when someone accepts the title "acting" administrator, others know that, for whatever reason, he doesn't want the job; he's a temporary fill-in until the permanent replacement arrives on the scene.

• Within your own institution, much the same attitude will prevail. You will be perceived as a messenger girl for one of your superiors, not as a responsible executive with authority in your own right. Your own staff will be hard to manage because you actually will have no more authority over them than you did last month when you were all equals. It's entirely possible that they may pay little or no attention to any orders you give because the superiors haven't invested you with any greater rank or status. And you may also discover that applicants whom you would like to hire are reluctant to take a job without knowing who the permanent boss will be.

• The debilitating effect on your own self-confidence won't show up for a while. Eventually, however, your anger will begin to surface and you'll berate yourself with all the questions you should be discussing with the chief before you finally accept the job. For instance: What is the purpose of the "acting" title? If you "don't work out," what prevents them from firing you just as they would anyone else whose performance is unsatisfactory? It is much better to be fired from a director's job than from a piddling little temporary post. Or do they expect you to take a six-month tryout as acting director and then cheerfully accept a demotion back to your writing job when they find a more suitable man? That's like putting another sign on yourself: "They Gave Me a Chance and I Failed."

• Above and beyond these personal difficulties is the broader issue: that you will represent all women executives because you will be the great Token Female in your institution. When nobody takes you seriously as public relations director, women who subsequently aim for administrative posts will be treated just as cavalierly. Tacking on that humiliating adjective to the title held by your male predecessor is demeaning your professional capability for this specific job while simultaneously separating the females from the males. Why don't you check back to see if any man ever started the job as acting director and was eventually promoted to director?

Before you finish negotiating for this promotion, you will have to pin down the money issue in actual dollars and cents. But the job title is your priority here. No amount of money will change any of the dangers you will create for yourself as a fly-by-night "acting" official.

Job titles pack a lot of meaning, much of it subliminal and much of it deliberately obfuscating to the uninitiated. It is interesting that your first response to a six-month public probation was: "That sounds fair."

I can't find anything "fair" about it.

This query had delightful consequences. It was one of those occasions when the questioner reported back on the outcome of the problematic situation. Nervous Nellie was nervous no longer; she was jubilant. "I got the job! Not quite as much money as I'd hoped but not too bad, $5,000 immediately and another $3,000 in six months."

She went to her department chief and, using the proffered arguments, explained how the acting title could prevent her from doing the best job. "He understood immediately," she said, "kept nodding his head, yes, yes, yes." He agreed absolutely that the announcement, her business cards, and any materials for public consumption would refer to her unequivocally as "Director." However, in the official personnel files she would be listed as "acting" because that (and this item she had not mentioned originally) would protect her union seniority if, for any reason, the promotion didn't work out.

Since the discussion was friendly and comfortable, she dared ask the chief why there were such persistent doubts about promoting her; after all, they knew she had adequate experience in the field, had appreciated the work she did over several years, knew her performance evaluations were consistently superior and that the ex-director recommended her. "Because you've never had any supervisory experience, here or at previous jobs. We don't know if you'll be able to handle a professional department." She counteracted that she's always had a secretary and sometimes other clerical assistants whom she's managed without difficulty. Then her boss revealed to her the hard management truth that many professional women, and as many secretaries, do not know. "Well, that doesn't count as supervisory experience—you just *tell* a secretary what to do."

# BLIND AMBITION

*Dear Betty Harragan:*

*A year and a half ago I was thrilled to be hired by a large bank to help develop profit-making services or properties. I had no banking experience but a good ten years' marketing background. My department, headed by one of the senior officers, was new and had a generous budget. My salary was excellent—and I've gotten a ten percent raise. Most of the time I've been working on one financial service product that everyone, including me, is anxious to introduce. It's a big responsibility, and doing it right requires information from people in operating and branch functions. However, I was told by my first boss not to "bother" managers at those levels. I considered that a ridiculous delaying tactic but I've encountered such obstacles before so I found roundabout ways to get the information without direct contact. I've also had to adjust to three different immediate bosses in this period, all of whom pressed me about the project but wouldn't give any help. Now it's almost done, and I've suddenly been informed that my department is being reorganized and I should look for another job (within the company if I want)—but first, turn in my project! I've been working madly, nights and weekends, to finish it but I wonder, "Where does responsibility as an employee end?" Especially when the whole atmosphere of the place is crazy.*

*Unbelieving*

Dear Unbelieving:

You put it rather colorfully, but several other women who switched from consumer organizations to banks or utilities have also told me they felt shock and disbelief at the ambivalence or indecisiveness of their new bosses.

Being a tightly regulated industry at national and state levels, banking in all its varieties falls into the conservative end of the business spectrum. Because so many overseer government agencies have a hand in bankers' operations, prudence has become the hallmark of their corporate thinking. To professionals used to the more demanding pace of customer-controlled companies (those which must respond promptly to consumer preferences), banks appear unbelievably stuffy, careful, methodical.

That tradition, however, is changing. Banking is being buffeted by the economic turbulence upsetting all industries; inflation and computer technology are demolishing tried-and-true practices. For the first time, banks face stiff competition from money market funds and brokerage firms. Regulatory restrictions are loosening gradually—but unevenly and unpredictably. Banking as an industry is in the midst of upheaval and in the process of transition.

These are some of the forces responsible for creating the job you got eighteen months ago. You have an expertise that was suddenly needed by your bank employer, who had no one to promote internally because aggressive marketing techniques were not previously practiced. (Much the same situation prevails in the newly separated divisions of the monolithic AT&T, and in other recently deregulated industries such as the airlines.) You were smart to take the job because new requirements in a changing business environment give women a chance to get a toehold. Nevertheless, you must realize that all innovative endeavors are in the nature of a gamble for both your employer and you. A new job like yours (that is, a heretofore nonexistent position) leaves much to the discretion of the job holder. You were in a situation where you could mold the job to your own specifications—but everything you did should have been calibrated to keep you in step with your employer's willingness to absorb the new operation. In short, you were in an extremely *political* situation.

How well you assessed what was going on around you, in the

larger organization, was far more important than the marketable product you were developing. Here's where you seemed to fall down. The excessive (and for a bank, unbelievably rapid) turnover of bosses should have warned you that your new department's ideas were not compatible with upper-management thinking. When you were further told *not* to consult with personnel who clearly had the know-how you lacked, that should have been a red flag to you. It was the equivalent of saying: "Hold everything. We've changed our minds or our priorities," and the signal for you to keep a low profile and let your beloved project simmer quietly on a back burner for a while.

Instead of interpreting these political cues correctly, you took the "ridiculous" hindrances as a challenge to your resourcefulness—and barreled ahead one way or another. In this approach, you resemble overwhelming numbers of conscientious women who focus all their attention on completing a specific task while neglecting to pay attention to the broader perspective of where the task fits within the company's or department's objectives. I can practically hear you protest, "But they *told* me to continue work on it; if the project wasn't wanted, that doesn't make sense!" Yes it does, once you analyze the situation.

Granting that the initial proposals from your floundering department were not immediately acceptable to senior officers, management continued to fund the *concept* of a marketing installation as a viable, if not inevitable, long-range need. You were on that experimental payroll so the only recourse for your immediate supervisors as they attempted to set some directions (unsuccessfully, as it turned out) was to tell you, "Keep on with whatever you're doing." They were less concerned with your immediate project than with keeping your salary line in the budget.

Your sudden notice to look for another job may mean that your employer has decided not to move so fast into a marketing stance—or it may mean that you blew your chance to get in on the ground floor of a slowly evolving framework. Whichever it was, you are fortunate in being offered a chance to find another niche within the bank's structure. I'd suggest you devote all your frustrated energies to that job hunt, trying to locate yourself where you can learn the basics of finance and the role of banking within it.

Your responsibility as an ambitious employee is to ferret out the underlying objectives and problems of your organization and to work within those constraints. Knocking yourself out to perfect a project that has been dead as a dodo for months is not in that class; it is more like worrying about ring-around-the-collar on a shirt that is ready for the rag bag. That's where "crazy" and "unbelieving" come into your story.

# RELOCATION

*Dear Betty Harragan:*

*I work for a retail jewelry chain and have done well during the past four years, getting promoted steadily. It is understood in this field that promotion depends heavily on a manager's willingness to relocate, an event that, in my company, occurs an average of three or four times a year. There is a big turnover in managers as a result, but since I'm single and unencumbered I've been able to move whenever necessary. In the past year alone I've been transferred twice to different states and now my boss has ordered another move. I just got settled in my present community, have joined some good business and sports clubs, and I hate to uproot myself so soon. My boss is pure Theory X—he issues orders and expects them to be obeyed without question if you want to get ahead here (which I do). His explanation for the latest transfer is, "We need you there." My question is: What effect does relocation have on one's future advancement? If I object to this move, will I have cut off chances for continued progress? I have a degree in business administration and don't want to muff any opportunities early in my career.*

*Cooperative*

Dear Cooperative:

You are right in recognizing that physical mobility and job mobility are closely connected at the middle-management level. It used to be a truism that an ambitious man who turned down a promotion because it involved relocation had effectively dead-ended himself. Ambitious women complained bitterly that they were not offered these promotions because their superiors assumed—without even asking!—that a woman wouldn't or couldn't move out of town.

In recent years, more women have been offered transfer-promotions (or have deliberately sought them out), resulting in occasional media stories about startling long-distance marriages. Unquestionably, there are growing numbers of mid-management women who understand that continued progress up the ladder depends, at certain points in their careers, on gaining experience in different geographic regions or far-flung plant sites. According to a survey by Management Woman, a division of Parker-Hyde Executive Search consultants in Greenwich, CT, sixty-six percent of single female executives and twenty-seven percent of married ones react positively to relocation opportunities. But a majority of women still turn down these offers for personal reasons—or rationalize that refusal to relocate will not harm their careers. Yet corporate managements and headhunters repeatedly cite such refusals as major obstacles in women's slow climb toward senior management positions. I see frequent evidence of the problem in my private consulting with stymied female executives; when a highly experienced woman with sound credentials is accepting an abnormally low salary, or having difficulty finding a better job, the reason can often be traced to her insistence: "But I don't want to leave New York"—or San Francisco, or Chicago, or Atlanta, or wherever she's entrenched.

Admittedly, when the woman has a husband who cannot move with her, plus young children, she has to weigh the pros and cons of her relocation very carefully. Sometimes the problem is insurmountable—she must give her primary allegiance to her family's welfare and gamble that another job opportunity will come her way in later years. But a surprising number of women resist geographic transfers for specious reasons: They just "like" the city they're in; all their friends or relatives live there; their boyfriends live nearby. These personal and emotional ties to a specific locale are not easily understood by bosses or human resource planners; some managements today can sympathize with realistic family obligations on the part of men as well as women, but not many appreciate undocumented excuses of "my wife doesn't want to move," or "my husband doesn't want me to move." Such explanations are taken as polite turndowns and get translated to the personnel file as "not interested in promotion," or "too inflexible for major responsibility."

In some companies, turning down a transfer is tantamount to quitting; you mention that there is a high turnover in managers in your company, so obviously your boss follows this precept. From your description, he is quite old-fashioned in his management style, operating from an authoritarian, if not tyrannical, base.

Granting that physical mobility is an important adjunct to serious high ambitions, relocation is not to be accepted lightly or uncritically. Sometimes it is used by ruthless bosses to exploit ambitious workers, and this may be what's happening to you. Organizations with well-planned relocation policies are well aware that such moves are expensive, so they ordinarily think in terms of years: one-year assignments at lower levels and two- to five-year assignments at higher managerial levels. In a retail outlet, a six-month stint might occasionally be feasible, but transferring store managers every few months is ridiculous from the employee's standpoint. How can anyone prove what she can do, or develop innovative buying, selling or marketing ideas in a couple of months? There is no way for a business executive to demonstrate managerial performance without reasonable time to analyze problems, plan new approaches, implement profitable methods and follow through on results. In other words, you are not being offered good managerial development with your boss's excessive transfer policy; you are being treated more like a store babysitter with dependable skills but without basic administrative responsibility.

I'd say it is time for you to pose the question you asked me— How will relocation affect my chances for advancement?—to the one who has the answer: your boss. By now you must have a pretty good track record with him and the company, so you could use this moment to discuss your future there. Find out what plans (if any) he has in mind for you and see if these dovetail with your own ambitions. Also discuss timing; you could transfer interminably and never move ahead, just laterally. The object of a promotion (with or without relocation) is to learn something new or to take on more significant responsibilities. Figure out if these frequent transfers are accomplishing that for you. His brusque explanation, "We need you there," immensely benefits him but not necessarily your career. What, for instance, happened to the previous manager? Is your boss playing musical chairs with employees for no discernible reason?

If he is "pure Theory X" he may not appreciate a subordinate's bringing up long-range policies, but you never know; maybe he'll be flattered and pleased at your obvious interest in his personnel problems. Before you talk to him, do your homework. List all the reasons that a transfer at this time will be counterproductive to your *job performance* (not your personal feelings). And while you're at it, check to see if the transfer histories of male managers are just as excessive as those for females. If not, you may be caught in the trap of separate, sex-segregated management tracks, where only the male pattern leads to senior management. In that case, it's time to transfer yourself to a different retail chain with more enlightened advancement policies and more progressive management.

## DEMOTION UNDER MERGER

*Dear Betty Harragan:*

*I just had an emotional blow-up with my boss, the director of development for a private university, because I'm getting demoted due to a reorganization. I threatened to see a lawyer, but I really want to keep my fifteen-year career on track. I've been here six years, and during the past three I've been director of public relations for development. It's an exciting job, and we've done well in a tough fund-raising market, so my performance evaluations are consistently good.*

*The problem arose because the public information departments of all campuses are now being consolidated into one office. I was notified that my title would be taken away and I'd report to a man who is head of public information on the main campus, where we'll all be relocated. My current boss fought the physical move, but he lost the battle. Now he seems indifferent to further changes, since he knows his title and function remain the same.*

*In addition to losing my title, I lose my staff, which will be melded with the other guy's staffs. Worst of all, I'll be subordinate to someone who has no experience in fund raising (which is significantly different from academic and scientific public-information work). Already the guy who will be my boss is asking me to show him what we do—effectively, to train him in my work. I'm furious at this insult, but I don't know what to do since I have no powerful connections. My current boss is marvelous at dealing with big donors, but he's a haphazard administrator and doesn't take internal affairs seriously.*

*As far as I can see, this entire college has no more than five female administrators (like the librarian and an assistant dean) among some fifty male officials. Am I right in thinking this is sex discrimination, when a less experienced male gets my job?*

*Distraught*

Dear Distraught:

You're probably right in seeing a typical pattern of discrimination following a consolidation. With this depressed economy, such mergers are occurring frequently, and seldom does the lone female get the combined position. That is one reason women's gains of the past few years are being severely checked.

By all means, keep investigating any and all aspects of sex discrimination in the overall institution, including evidence of salary discrepancies. I would bet that the man getting the consolidated title is making far more than you, even though you supposedly were on identical levels. Technically you should make more because you're part of an income-producing department, rather than the expense function the PI director is in. Yet the fact that he was picked as head man indicates his higher salary; to give you the top job would necessitate a huge jump in your salary, because one cannot have subordinates who make far more than the boss. When the chips are down, the one with the higher salary will always be the first considered for expanded responsibility or promotion. I cannot emphasize enough to women that fighting for *equal* salary is the most important element in their career development; the rungs of the upward mobility ladder are made only of dollars.

Be that as it may, your immediate problem needs immediate attention—and these days a sex-discrimination charge must be viewed as a long-range, carefully plotted strategy to undo past wrongs (it takes years even to process one, much less prosecute it). Keep building your case, but let's see what else you can do to avoid so drastic a step. You think you have no "powerful connections," but you do have one important colleague whose future will be as much affected by this move as yours—your present boss, head of the money-raising operations. He's bound to have clout if he's intimate with big donors; that's a "job skill" he can merchandise anywhere. Little wonder his title and position remain intact; he's almost indispensable.

On the other hand, you say he's a poor administrator and doesn't take your situation seriously. Perhaps there is a way to make him see how serious it is. Look at the proposed change from his point of view. Under the consolidation plan, he will lose his support staff, because you will all now report to somebody else! In other words, your boss is also being demoted in a sense. Does he see that? From now on, he'll be put in the position of repeatedly begging another department head for loan of that executive's people, in place of having a crew of fund-raising specialists to himself.

I'm sure he's been assured that all he has to do is call on the combined department for adequate servicing of the fund-raising operation, so you'll have to dramatize to him how this scheme will work in everyday practice. For example, in a consolidated department you and your writers will undoubtedly be looked upon as generalists who can be assigned to any necessary tasks; the top honcho will naturally assume that the work he presently does, and is familiar with, deserves priority over another's work (the development director's), so your present boss may have to fight constantly to get as much production and flexibility as he's used to. There's no guarantee he'll get fund-raising specialists; he may have to settle for any writers who have the time.

If your present boss and the new public information head are not very compatible types (and I doubt it, if the campus man doesn't even know what the development director's staff does), the inevitable conflict over time allotment will eventually have to be decided by a higher official. So there's your boss, crying and complaining to superiors that he can't get his work processed! I can't believe he would walk into such a potential hornet's nest if he'd given it serious thought. He'll be reduced to a level below the PI head in status. Your best move is to bring all this to his attention. Other relevant arguments may be raised. What, for instance, is the practice in the industry? Do other development directors have hollow titles, reigning over one-person departments with no subordinate support staff? What kind of personality does your boss have? Will he gladly subdue his own ego and self-importance to explain his needs to a lateral executive who controls the workload of his former staff?

I can't see any evidence here of saving money or increasing efficiency by combining two distinct specialties, inasmuch as all the employees are being retained. White-collar professionals require the same office and overhead investment, whether assigned to one boss or another. Apparently the only beneficiary is the guy who instantly doubles or triples his department size and gains absolute control over anyone who calls upon the services of his enlarged staff. It's obvious that you, personally, will be put in an intolerable situation.

From every practical viewpoint, this ill-considered plan stands no chance of success. Before you do anything else, sit down with your current boss and lay out this whole scenario of what it will mean to *him*, not you. Once you outline the internal political ramifications, he ought to see that his only recourse is to insist that his existing department, with titles undisturbed, be moved intact as a continuing part of his function. Then hand him his trump card: Say that you foresee fund-raising activities getting more complex and intense under present economic conditions, so his department may have to expand, not shrink, just to achieve past levels of giving.

If your boss doesn't respond to these arguments, he's a lost cause—or he's in cahoots with university management to harass you out and justify giving your job to a less-qualified male. In which case your discrimination charge could be viable.

# CHAPTER SIX

# Back to School

## CHANGING CAREERS

*Dear Betty Harragan:*
*I recently quit my promising job to return to school full time. My husband strongly disapproves of my decision, which he calls "a suicidal career move." We need expert advice to settle our arguments. After six years with a major insurer, I had risen from entry-level clerk to head of a pension unit. I was being groomed for larger responsibilities, including another promotion within a year, through rotating assignments and managerial experience on special team projects. My three bosses up the line were most encouraging and, when I quit, said I'd always be welcomed back. But I want to get a master's degree in English and enter the academic world where I can teach at a small college and write, since my main interest is literature. I quit college years ago, so I face at least a five-year undergraduate/graduate study program. I think education offers a broader perspective and can only enhance my chances for finding work closer to my interests. My husband, who is a Ph.D. and director of a scientific laboratory, insists that life is the best education and I shouldn't count on executives' glowing exit promises. I feel sure that if economic considerations should disrupt my schooling, I can easily*

*return to pension work, a field where I am extremely competent but largely indifferent. I'm 35 with a young child and "fell into" my first career; now I'm planning one.*

*Happy Student*

Dear Happy:

There's much to be said for any move which makes one happy. Very likely you have regretted whatever impelled you to drop out of college and now feel you are partly recapturing some of that lost youth. On a realistic level, these days it is essential for an aspiring executive to have a bachelor's degree. From that viewpoint, your decision to complete your education has merit.

However, that's the advice you needed when you were a teenager; as an adult, you have to weigh far more complex factors, and I suspect some of these provoke the disagreements with your husband. No Ph.D. would discount the value of university credentials; but once you've established a foothold on a career ladder, theoretical book learning depreciates rapidly. In a very real sense academic degrees are like tickets purchased at the box office allowing entry into beginners' professional jobs. If one fortunately gets into an on-the-job training program (as you obviously did in the pension field), this is the business equivalent of postgraduate schooling—and every bit of it is immediately applicable as well as being prerequisite to more advanced management "courses." In game terms, you "Advance to Go" without the preliminary college ticket.

That kind of job luck is transitory for women; it will probably not be duplicated in the future as employers demand college degrees in place of once-acceptable high school diplomas. Your husband senses this even though he explains it rather vaguely as "life is the best education." His business antennae confirm your statement that the company was definitely grooming you for significant advancement—so your sudden regression to by-now-irrelevant book learning strikes him as "career suicide." I must say I agree. You have dropped out of real-life management school just as surely as you dropped out of college many years ago. This propensity for opting out does not augur well for success in your present endeavor, which involves a tough, grinding commitment to years of dull required courses, stressful tests, endless research and strictly monitored dissertations.

Your approach to career decision-making is extremely important because it mirrors an internal conflict that is tearing apart millions of ambitious women. Indeed, your problem is a "female-conditioning" classic. You pose your dilemma as Job (accidental achievement) vs. Education (happiness); in actuality your choice is between economic independence and "ladylike" pursuits.

You sincerely believe that you are "planning" a more suitable second career. Planning is a rigorous intellectual exercise that requires accumulation of hard data about the occupation you've identified, as well as evaluation of the factual and personal pros and cons to decide whether the result is desirable as well as achievable. You present no evidence of such concrete investigation.

Without doing your research for you, let me cite a few widely known, broadly publicized facts about the occupation: College English Teacher. Ph.D.'s in the humanities (especially English) have glutted the market since the early 1970s. Those few who manage to get permanent appointments at the lowest instructor grade find salaries range from $8,000 to $12,000 a year, but the growing trend among financially strapped colleges is to hire part-time, temporary adjunct professors who are paid by the course and are lucky to gross $1,000 to $4,000 a year. The predictions for the mid-1980s are progressively worse! This is the *career* you are planning? M.A.'s don't even count in this ridiculously competitive arena. At best you might command a top academic salary at age fifty that is half your present income—without, of course, any fringes, benefits, pensions or promotion prospects.

If I were you, I would run to the nearest reference library and check all the occupational-outlook handbooks; then talk to all your classroom teachers and ask them what their job title, salary, future and tenure status is. Don't feel that you are alone in your confusion. You represent the majority of all female college students today: seventy-two percent of master's degrees and fifty-six percent of doctorates earned by women are in such traditional "feminine" fields as English or journalism, nursing and education—traditionally low-paid, dead-end occupations regardless of the advanced education entailed. For women, formal education never translates to comparable workforce dollars. To get the unvarnished truth about conditions in academia (faculty and students), write to the Project on the Status and Education of Women, Association of American Colleges, 1818 R Street, NW, Washington, D.C. 20009. Its quarterly news journal, "On Campus with Women," plus topical papers, is a bargain for individuals at $15 a year, and an indispensable information resource for all those interested in the academic field or planning to reenter college.

Meanwhile, I'd suggest you get back to the pension field fast, before you lose too much momentum (you'll find out quickly enough whether executive promises are dependable). Then continue your studies in night school. If you are really good at writing, there is a way to combine your hobby with your salaried career job—and become world famous in the process. Just produce one clear, readable, grammatical, interesting and technically accurate article about E.R.I.S.A.!

(For the uninitiated, E.R.I.S.A. is the acronym for the Employee Retirement Income Security Act, the massive federal pension law that has been called the most complicated and incomprehensible piece of legislation ever written; its existence is responsible for the explosive demand for pension specialists since 1974. To further confuse the subject, the Tax Equity and Fiscal Responsibility Act of 1982—known as T.E.F.R.A.—has ordered sweeping changes in E.R.I.S.A. that affect all types of pension/retirement plans.)

As might be expected, the proponents of "learning and scholarship" over "illiterate business vocational schooling" rose up to defend Happy Student, with whom they fully sympathized. Others chimed in to support women's right to make career decisions based on "personal satisfaction and enjoyment" rather than the values of the marketplace.

I have no disagreement with those viewpoints providing they are sincere. Many people pursue liberal arts studies or follow scholarly bents throughout their lifetime because they are genuinely interested in a specific subject or in continued intellectual development. Today, some of the top universities are revamping class schedules to compete with community colleges in accommodating adult night students who work in unrelated fields during the day. In fact, that option was open to Happy

Student to assuage her longing for literary studies—*if* that was her goal. But it wasn't; she was contemplating college teaching as a vocation. That's a different issue.

Choosing or changing careers is an important subject; it deserves as much attention as analyzing a Shakespearean sonnet. I wanted her to look behind the facade of her devotion to literary scholarship—beyond her romantic Victorian vision of a small secluded college where she could indulge her daydream of reading and writing in an ivory tower (and get paid to do it). That picture bears no relation to college teaching as it exists today. If personal satisfaction is what she's after, she has as good a chance of achieving it by staying in the pension business, which is probably less stressful and demanding than jobs in higher education. Absent-minded professors aren't a growth industry outside of British historical novels. The marketplace has invaded the groves of academe.

Where that marketplace juxtaposes with student interests is in the business and management schools, especially the much-touted M.B.A. (Master of Business Administration) programs. At times it seems as if all ambitious women who've hit a snag in their careers consider "going back to get an M.B.A." Obviously the excessive publicity about fabulous salaries offered to certain B-school graduates acts as a siren lure to women who have plateaued at positions with little future. They furtively eye M.B.A. programs as magic carpets that will whisk them up the managerial ladder. Succumbing to this heady expectation can be as risky a form of career planning as dedication to the dying humanities. For some job-holders, earning an M.B.A. is a worthwhile move; for many others it is an expensive indulgence that adds very little cash value in the open market. Notice how many ramifications of their decisions the following women failed to consider.

*Dear Betty Harragan:*

*I am a classic case—a woman who graduated in 1965 with a degree in secondary education. After teaching junior high for four years, I transferred to state government where I advanced steadily in the hierarchy for the next ten years. About five years ago I began to understand my own need to achieve. I wanted power, influence, money and recognition. I wanted a career objective and plan. I wanted to be part of the mysterious and fascinating world of corporate management.*

*Such desires did not elicit approval from my husband or the men and women in my world. They couldn't understand why I wasn't content with a good job and salary. My dissatisfaction grew until I decided to get an M.B.A. degree. First I had to take preparatory math courses because my quantitative education had stopped at tenth grade. Now I'm about to graduate from a respected eastern university with an M.B.A. concentration in finance. On the one hand, I am exhilarated and assured because I have proved to myself that I can learn, and am as capable as those I used to envy. On the other hand, I am suddenly not at all confident. I was described by a management recruiter as a "square peg," and he said he was looking for round pegs to fit his corporation's round holes. Why must I be seen as a square peg because I am a thirty-seven-year-old woman taking control of her life? How do I remove this barrier to the corporate world?*

*Pegged*

Dear Pegged:

I'm afraid you pointed to the crux of the problem with your stated desire to become part of "the mysterious and fascinating world of corporate management." Fascinating it may be (although that's debatable), but mysterious it is not. The requirements for getting a foot on the managerial ladder are more or less explicit, at least from a corporate recruiter's viewpoint. A little sober reflection might have tempered your earlier enthusiasm, or at least fore-warned you that the "square peg" designation loomed ahead.

Your approach to graduate education neglected a significant item: that you hoped to *change careers* with this move. Your entire fourteen-year background is in government service (public school teachers are also employees of local governments), yet you expected two years' additional education would prepare you for corporate management. That's a drastic shift in direction, from the nonprofit to the profit environment. Private industry looks upon it as a different game, somewhat comparable to a long-time baseball in-fielder wanting to play on a professional basketball team because the court game looks more fascinating and mysterious. Certain players might effectuate such a transfer eventually if they have the physique and adaptability for a much faster pace—but they'd still have to learn the game of basketball. To do that, they'd have to start on a rookie team until they showed the requisite proficiency to move on to more skilled teams.

Much the same applies to changing careers. By earning an M.B.A. degree you learned the rudiments of the profit-industry game; therefore, at graduation you are eligible to compete with other graduates for a spot on the rookie business teams. You have entry credentials but you don't yet have any proven skills. Schooling, after all, is just book-learning. Good marks show you have absorbed the lessons, but an employer has no way of knowing whether you (or anybody else) can *apply* those lessons in a job setting. Just like the baseball player, you have to demonstrate your proficiency from the rookie level up—in other words, beginning with an entry level or trainee job. If you prove successful, and have whatever other qualifications are deemed important, you may gradually be offered additional challenges, i.e., be promoted.

Proving proficiency on the job takes time (in the vernacular, it's called "experience"). Corporate recruiters are supersensitive to justifying their decisions so they look for a combination of qualities that presage good potential—plus *time* to develop that potential. "Time" is calculated as approximately 20 years because it's widely assumed that is how long it takes to groom a corporate executive for senior management posts. Statistical profiles tend to buttress the opinion of search consultants that by age forty it is clear whether a man has succeeded or failed in the managerial competition. Men who have progressed steadily in responsibility and income during the previous ten to twenty years will probably continue to move ahead; those who have been sidetracked or slowed down for some reason have probably reached the end of their "potential." Women as a group aren't reflected in these statistical profiles because so few women were on the rookie teams even five or ten years ago. Nobody can tell how they'll stack up since only a handful have accumulated the typical twenty years of essential experience. (The few who have are looking good!)

That's why the recruiter called you a square peg: you are ten to fifteen years behind the timetable for developing your hard-earned potential. This is not to say age thirty-seven is old; it merely acknowledges that this is a late age to start as a rank beginner in corporate managerial training. If your prior experience had been in private industry, your M.B.A. could be viewed as "filling out" or expanding your knowledge to qualify you for broader managerial responsibility. Come to think of it, fifteen years of solid managerial progression would probably mean you don't need an M.B.A. You'd be in a position to hire newly graduated M.B.A.s to handle whatever number-crunching you needed done. A lot of non-M.B.A. corporate managers are adopting this technique. They simply reevaluate a job that was previously ranked as high-level clerical and attach an M.B.A. credential, thereby upping the status of their department by boasting about the number of M.B.A.s they supervise. Your view of these cute management tricks was "fascinating," I believe?

Age might be a less significant factor in boom times, but a recessionary or slow-growth economy exaggerates its importance. Today, demand for M.B.A. credentials is not keeping pace with the escalating number of yearly graduates. In 1982 some 56,000 M.B.A. degrees were awarded and those numbers have been increasing steadily over the past few years as more and more colleges join the estimated 500 M.B.A. schools. (That's the marketplace operating in academia: if M.B.A. degrees attract tuition, that's what colleges will offer even though a goodly percentage of the business programs are not accredited.) In addition to M.B.A. graduate schools, there are rapidly expanding undergraduate programs in business and management, many of whose graduates compete with M.B.A.s for the same corporate trainee slots.

With that depressing litany out of the way (primarily for the benefit of other M.B.A. hopefuls who should weigh the negatives as well as the positives before embarking on this degree program), you are in a position to judge your own prospects more realistically. You *are* a square peg, so your best bet is to seek a square hole where you fit rather than jam yourself into some misshapen round hole. Essentially that means you will have to forage in the marketplace for your own job. Most M.B.A. professionals, as well as lawyers, have to do that anyway in this restricted labor market. Those high-paying M.B.A. jobs the media loves to headline are generally limited to the top-ranking students from prestigious schools. The vast majority of business/management graduates go shopping for jobs on their own, and often settle for much less than their grandiose expectations.

In assessing your job options, a good case could be made for returning to your original field—government. This would capitalize on your past experience instead of negating it. Admittedly, government is not a growth industry at the moment, but the same economic constraints that are reducing employment are creating a demand for specialists with financial, analytical skills. Some beleaguered public agencies, for the first time in history, are looking to the management expertise developed by private industry to help them reorganize decimated programs or to utilize shrunken funding in more effective ways. Where such openings exist (or where you could persuade an agency to create one), you can be sure they are not beginner's jobs; they would be consequential administrative posts.

The grass is not always greener when one hurdles the fence. To many in private industry, the arena of government administration looks as mysterious and fascinating as their management world looks to you. Inside, on a day-to-day performance basis, they are no longer so different—primarily because money has become the guiding star in both instances.

*Dear Betty Harragan:*

*Is pursuing a Ph.D. the most appropriate preparation for entering the field of Industrial Psychology as a consultant with special interests in communication, arbitration and the integration of women into management? What arenas of specializations will be in greatest demand during the next ten to fifteen years? I am thirty-seven, got a B.A. in management in 1979, have always been self-employed helping my husband run a camp seventy miles from the nearest urban center. I will need financial assistance to return to school and set up a separate residence. I am experiencing strong resistance from my spouse on this career shift. I feel this letter is the "homework" you recommend women do.*

*California*

Dear California:

Sorry, that's not quite what I mean by doing "homework" on the pros and cons of shifting careers. I'm beginning to notice that many husbands are offering accurate, pragmatic appraisals of the real world to counter their wives' idealistic career notions, but the women refuse to accept the truth. They take hard-nosed advice as a manifestation of male resistance to a woman's self-actualization. Surely that occurs in some marriages, but just as surely there are facts that must be faced before creating upheavals in one's life to chase ephemeral goals.

"Homework" on career options inevitably starts in the public library, the bigger the better. The starting point is consulting two huge tomes put out by the U.S. Department of Labor: *The Dictionary of Occupational Titles* (known as the *D.O.T.*) and the *Occupational Outlook Handbook*, plus updates in the *Occupational Outlook Quarterly*. These basic references will tell the uninitiated whether an occupation exists and what work it entails. For example, there is no job listing in *D.O.T.* for "industrial psychologist," although there are over a dozen psychologist jobs in assorted subcategories, and one consultant title with a limitless range of client service designations. The 1982–1983 edition of the *Outlook Handbook* describes what the work is like, the job prospects to 1990, qualifications, training and educational requirements, working conditions, related occupations, earnings, and advancement opportunities, plus sources for additional information.

Then you should consult the *Periodicals Index* to find current magazine and journal articles in your field of interest, and finally, the mammoth list of *Books in Print* to get the titles of hundreds of recent books dealing with jobs and careers for women. Many career counselors suggest that you locate people in the field you're investigating and ask them what they do every day, how they like it, etc. In my experience that mechanism has dubious value unless you have thoroughly indoctrinated yourself about the field beforehand. No specific job (with the possible exception of unskilled labor) is so one-dimensional that a single practitioner can give you a representative picture of the work. The other weakness in personal interviews is that the totally naive don't grasp half of what the experienced professional is telling them; the most gracious explanations often fall on deaf ears.

Once you've saturated yourself in information about the field and jobs within it, the next step is checking out the educational requirements and the institutions that offer the best programs. This is another library chore: checking college and university catalogues, evaluations of schools, success records of graduates, time requirements and, of course, financial considerations. Around this stage you should be able to make an *informed* decision about the validity of your chosen career in light of your personal circumstances and your personality attributes.

Under those circumstances, if you decide to go ahead you will be very successful. You'll know what you're doing and won't be shocked when inevitable difficulties crop up along the way. But if you just stumble around in the morass of perpetual education, you may be severely disappointed on the career front. There's no need for blind plunges into vacuous career paths; the most isolated of individuals have access to some library resources and helpful, trained librarians.

# RETURNING FOR DEGREES

*Dear Betty Harragan:*

*I'm 28, single, trying to relocate in another state. I've worked for a retail chain the past five years, rising from administrative assistant to personnel administrator. I have a personnel certificate from a two-year college but I don't have a B.A. My problem is that companies are requiring a bachelor's degree plus five years' related experience.*

*Frustrated*

*I'm 34, with a preschool child. I dropped out of college in my junior year to get married. I have a minor managerial job. Without a degree I don't get in the door of places that pay at least forty percent more than I'm now earning. Our local college doesn't offer night degree programs in business, and I can't afford to quit work to attend school in a distant city. Are there any alternatives?*

Stymied

*I'm twenty-two and hope someday to be chairman of the board of a large corporation. There are, however, a few stumbling blocks in my path. I left college after two years and am told I don't qualify for management training positions because I don't have a B.A. or a B.S. I intend to use my employer's tuition reimbursement plan to complete my undergraduate work and go on for a graduate degree in marketing. Meanwhile, how can I move from a clerical to a "line" position?*

Thwarted

Dear Dropouts:

Judging by my mail, there are two topics of overwhelming concern to ambitious women: How to get the job you want and how to return to college. Naturally, there is considerable overlap between these subjects, since earning undergraduate or graduate degrees is generally tied to aspirations for a better job or more satisfactory occupation.

On general principles, I advise women to investigate carefully and be very selective when considering a return to college after a long hiatus. This warning is necessary because many women are easy prey for Go-Back-To-School pitches; they blindly presume that a college degree per se will automatically entitle them to a more lucrative or more "executive" job. Sorry, but that's not how the scholastic chips stack up. The relationship between college degrees and jobs is far more complicated and usually quite indirect. This is especially true of graduate or advanced degrees.

On the other hand, there is one time when it is mandatory to return to school: when you have dropped out of college and have no bachelor's degree. One offshoot of women's unprecedented influx into the paid workforce is that employers are inflating the formal education requirements even for menial jobs. That means that an undergraduate degree seldom qualifies you for a "better" job, but it will remove an otherwise insurmountable obstacle. In effect, a baccalaureate degree has become the *sine qua non* these days for almost any job above unskilled ranks. (There are plenty of lousy jobs in the skilled professional/managerial categories, so never overestimate the increments in either salary or status that flow from a bachelor's degree.)

A major problem when returning to school is getting your earlier college courses accredited. As "Frustrated" found out, a two-year certificate is virtually worthless except to accumulate prerequisite credits for subsequent study. Unfortunately for reentry students, many credits earned at one school (whether a two- or four-year college) are not readily accepted by another one. Each educational institution sets its own policies on transfer credits and these decisions are influenced by time (how long out of school), marks earned, outmoded subjects, revised major requirements, academic rating of the former school, idiosyncracies of the dean, and a host of other objective and subjective criteria. The point is, you should shop around and bargain with various colleges to get the best deal possible for yourself. There's no sense in losing full years of prior schooling or repeating elementary subjects if you can avoid it.

In that regard, all reentry candidates should look into the standardized tests that give credit for "life experience" or off-campus learning. The best known of these are the C.L.E.P. Tests (College Level Examination Programs) given by the College Entrance Examination Board. By passing a series of examinations in general areas (humanities, natural sciences, English composition, etc.) or examinations in specific subjects, you may be able to get credit for certain required courses, or at least be exempted from taking courses in subject matter you already know. You might be surprised how smart you are! Be sure to discuss these (and other) "testing out" possibilities with your various college choices. New York State actually has a program—The Regents External Degree Program of the University of the State of New York—wherein you can earn certain baccalaureate degrees entirely by test, without ever studying on campus. Other state universities and colleges are moving in this direction so it's worth a little serious investigation.

Don't feel stymied if nearby schools have no night programs in the discipline you want; shift to whatever is offered that's closely related. If you can't complete a business degree part time, see if you can arrange a major in economics, math, accounting or one of the pure sciences. Just steer away from degrees in English or philosophy or nonprofit vocational training such as education or social work, which offer no immediate monetary rewards.

While pursuing a delayed undergraduate education, it's important to keep working and to progress as far as you can. When lack of a degree keeps you in the clerical ranks, look for secretarial or assistant jobs working for a respected executive in the field you've chosen. Any on-the-job learning you acquire will ultimately benefit you more than esoteric schooling. I know that sounds contradictory, but extended withdrawal from the workforce (for whatever reason) is hard to overcome. Besides, there seems to be an unwritten rule that the years between 18 and 24 are reserved for undergraduate schooling; going against the tide marks you as a dilettante.

Yes, I agree that's crazy—and very unfair to women. But as of now, that's the way industry looks at it.

*Dear Betty Harragan:*

*There's another solution to this dilemma, one I wish I had used and may still use if the opportunity presents itself.*

*I have no degree. I started out in one of the Fortune top ten in a clerical position and in my mid-twenties talked my way into a marketing representative job. To everyone's amazement, I was very good at it and in the subsequent ten years was promoted from the field to a headquarters job for exposure and experience, then transferred back to the field in a management capacity and am now ready for a significant promotion. But I'm faced with the fact that my next step to middle-management will be my last—unless I do something about my education. A little bit of larceny would have fixed this years ago. Each time I relocated it would have been simple to have the computer change my educational status on my profile. Instant degree. Why didn't I think of it then?*

*Thoughtless*

Dear Thoughtless:

No, no, no, no! You can fudge or stretch the facts on almost anything in a resume or job profile *except* where you worked and where you were awarded a degree. All colleges and universities seem to keep impeccable records on their graduates, if for no other reason than to dun alumni for donations and bequests forever after. Employers also keep capsule records on past employees and dates of employment. It's almost impossible to get away with claiming you worked somewhere you never worked, or graduated from some school where you earned no degree.

At this stage in your upward climb nobody is apt to check such mundane background items. However, as you continue on this fast track, you'll get into the arena where the boys play hardball. If and when your advancement becomes a threat to someone, or you get entangled in a competitive political scene, one of your corporate enemies may go looking for any weakness in your background or record. If it turned up that you lied about your education, that could be a time bomb to destroy you. It's the lying, not the lack of education, that's dangerous. For no reason I can fathom, lying about educational degrees is considered an ultimate sin—probably because most of the private universities started out as religious institutions, or maybe because colleges and universities would be hard put to identify who finished college and who didn't unless they put an irrevocable brand on each degree recipient.

Don't fool around with this one. Gather up your determination, take all the advanced placement tests available, and start plugging along nights and weekends to get this chore over with. Before your next promotion see if you can wrangle a subsidized leave and use it to overload credits during one or two full-time terms. You'll probably find undergraduate class work a cinch and enjoyable. You are in the unique position of majoring in any subject you like because all you need are those elusive initials: B.A. (Or would you prefer B.S.?)

# CHAPTER SEVEN

# Confronting Money

## WHAT ARE THE RISKS?

Money, money, money.

That, the man said, is what makes the world go round. Most certainly it is the topic that should be foremost in the minds of all working women if we ever hope to alter the appalling, unchanging reality that full-time employed women are paid about sixty percent of the salary paid to full-time working men in the same occupation with the same experience and education. Don't ever fool yourself that just because you have a Ph.D., an M.D., an LL.B., an M.E.E. or an M.B.A. that you are being paid equally. The underpayment of women in this society is so pervasive that the rarity is the isolated woman here or there who temporarily gets the same compensation as a male peer.

The causes of this relentless wage gap between male and female salaries are complex. Job segregation is the major villain. That's the monster being tackled by the "comparable pay" or "pay equity" precept, i.e., why is the kind of work traditionally done by women (nurses, secretaries, etc.) worth less in dollars and cents than the kinds of work traditionally done by men (parking lot attendants, garbagemen, etc.). Entrenched societal attitudes that are historically antifemale, and hoary job evaluation systems that are inherently discriminatory, help perpetuate the discrepancy. But even in fields that are comparatively integrated (as are most of the examples in this chapter), the inequality in pay continues.

Individual working women bear a certain amount of responsibility for this unconscionable state of affairs. Women must train themselves—and force themselves—to confront the subject of money at every turn, especially as it concerns their salary, raises, benefits, bonuses, pensions, insurance and taxes. It doesn't matter how much or how little education you have, you can learn about money. Math anxiety, by the way, is no excuse because math has to do with algebra, calculus or similar numerical abstractions. Money, however, is a simple scoring tool in the games of business. Anyone who earns it should be able to count it—and know when she's short-changed.

Negotiating for equal pay and appropriate increases is a primary career game skill that demands continual practice. If women are loathe to develop adroitness in this arena, their chances of cultivating finesse are not good. Discussions with your boss about money matters should be as frequent as possible. That doesn't mean you bring up your salary every day, but do take advantage of openings to talk about the economy, the company's financial state, the local job market, the significance of budget allocations, rumors of cutbacks or expansions, the rate of inflation, any costs of doing business.

The point in such self-imposed drill is to become comfortable with the subject of money in all its ramifications. When you can talk about money openly and freely—and relate it to the economic module of your workplace—then discussions about your salary reevaluation or raises are part of a piece, not annual life-and-death confrontations so terrifying to contemplate that they are usually avoided. My own estimate, based on informal surveys of thousands of ambitious women around the country, is that ninety percent have never asked for a raise. Consequently, they are leaving their financial present and future to fate. And fate, in this context, invariably means the lowest possible compensation package.

For a host of reasons (some personal and some fallacious logic), women are fearful about broaching the subject of salary and raises. They look upon such discussions as putting their job in jeopardy—taking an enormous risk. In fact, the risks are all in the opposite direction; an employee's value to an institution is measured in dollars and cents (like it or not) so the major risk to a woman's advancement is being underpaid for the work she does. No matter how good her performance, her achievements will be mentally discounted to the level of her relative salary.

A couple of years ago I witnessed a remarkable demonstration of the divergent views held by women and men in relation to this topic. It was the closing session of a three-day management conference for women. The featured guest was a male senior executive in the same profession. Just prior to his speech, the president of the association asked the audience what they had gained from the weekend seminars. One woman rose to say, "The most important thing I discovered is that I'm underpaid. I intend to go back to the office and immediately ask for a raise." The audience nodded eagerly, in full agreement. "Even," she concluded nervously, "if I get fired for it!"

At that, the other women broke into wild applause. Clearly she was expressing the deep-seated fears of her female associates in her assessment of the dangers, as well as gaining admiration for her determination to proceed with this hazardous undertaking. When the male guest took the podium he was admittedly in a state of shocked bewilderment. Departing from his prepared text, he said he couldn't help but comment on the preceding dialogue:

"I've held executive or management positions in this field for more years than I care to count. Yet this is the first time I ever heard anyone equate asking for a raise with getting fired. In my experience the person who asks for a raise gains added respect—whether he or she gets the raise or not. Bosses I've known, including myself, generally respect the individual who can evaluate a job well done and relate performance to salary. Frankly, I've never known anybody to get fired for requesting a raise."

What working women regard as a risk, men treat as a fail-safe gamble: If you don't get the raise, you at least gain respect from superiors. (And next time around, as you improve your bartering skills, you will no doubt get the raise.)

Salary, important as it is, is but one of the money items that must be dealt with in the course of a lifetime career. Expense accounts, I discovered, are another issue that dramatically separates women from men. When I got the first hesitant query on this topic I made a serious miscalculation. Coming from a twenty-year background in jobs with a discretionary expense account, I thought "Who doesn't know this?" and set aside the letter as not widely representative of women's problems. But the question nagged me and I began to ask women displaying American Express cards if they ever had trouble over expense accounts. I was stunned by the depths of anxiety, confusion and anger my casual comment exposed. All women, it seems, have ambivalent feelings about expense accounts and I realized that I had not always made intelligent use of expenses over the years. Here was a money subject I was as ready as anybody to sweep under the carpet; it was time to address it. Originally I hoped to collect tips from executive women with substantial travel and expense allowances to pass on to the less experienced. But when two of my prime candidates—seemingly confident women in high managerial jobs—said, "The less I spend, the better I look," I knew that the only dependable sources of accurate information on these practices remain men—successful men in high executive positions. We women still have a long, long way to go in grasping the critical nuances of money in the contemporary work world.

## WATCH YOUR STARTING SALARY

*Dear Betty Harragan:*

*I recently discovered that a male colleague hired with me four years ago makes $10,000 more than I do. I love this company, the marketing work and the people, but now I'm utterly disillusioned. I have an excellent record (got a $5,000 raise and title change after my first year) and have increased my salary from $16,000 to $25,000. I asked my boss for a $10,000 raise this year to equal my male associate, but he said his superiors were adamant that the best they could do was $2,000 to $3,000, and that "was stretching the seven percent guidelines." Nobody denied I was underpaid; they just said their hands were tied and it was unfortunate that I started too low. What can I do?*

*Disillusioned*

Dear Disillusioned:

If it were any comfort (which it isn't) I'd say, "Welcome to the club." You are caught in a trap that snares the majority of advancing women. Don't be too fast to blame your company; that may not be where the fault lies. Let's analyze how this wage gap could have developed within a company which tried to be fair and unbiased.

I suspect you were thrilled in 1980 when you got this exciting job because it gave you a chance to demonstrate your ability and you felt sure you could then move ahead on merit. When the company offered $16,000, you grabbed it, eagerly, gratefully, and determined to prove your future worth. Obviously you did, since you got a whopping raise after the first year's trial period and substantial increases since.

About the same time four years ago your associate was probably offered the same $16,000—but he didn't jump at it. He understood that every intelligent boss will try to hire newcomers at the lowest possible salary, so he assumed that the offering figure was at the low end of the salary scale. He took it upon himself to negotiate that figure upwards, aiming for the middle or upper quadrant of the range. Like you, he figured this job as a launching pad once he'd proved his ability, but meanwhile he wanted to launch from the best financial position possible.

Apparently he's quite persuasive (marketing-minded?) because it looks like he got the initial offer upped some $5,000 or $6,000, in which case he'd have started at $21,000 to $22,000. After the trial year he no doubt got the same thirty percent merit raise you did— with one significant difference. His raise brought his salary to $28,000, which was beyond the range of the original job classification, so he had to be moved into the next higher category. (Your clue about the "title change" tipped me off that he must have negotiated a high starting salary compared to you, especially since a range of $15,000 to $22,000 would not be unusual at your professional level.)

If not for him, you might not have received that early "promotion" because your salary—even after the first big raise—didn't break through the top of the range. Nonetheless, your company promoted you too—not merely because you deserved it, but because your salary hit the high end of one range and could be squeaked into the lowest end of the next (there is usually a slight salary overlap in successive job classifications). Assuming you both

got the same percentage raises in following years, here's how your
salary patterns look:

|      | You | | Him |
|------|------|------|------|
|      | *You* | | *Him* |
| 1980 | $16,000 | | $22,000 |
|      | + 5,000 | (30%) | + 6,600 |
| 1981 | 21,000 | | 28,600 |
|      | + 2,100 | (10%) | + 2,900 |
| 1982 | 23,100 | | 31,500 |
|      | + 2,300 | (10%) | + 3,150 |
| 1983 | $25,400 | | $34,650 |

You're right about the wage differential; he's close to $35,000
and you're nearer $25,000 by now. Incidentally, no percentage-
increase arithmetic can be precise because many smaller companies
tend to "round off" a raise to the nearest hundred or thousand
dollars, whereas large corporations are apt to computerize down to
the last cent.

The guidelines your boss mentioned refer to the salary or raise
restraints many employers have adopted to hold down their labor
costs during the recession. Companies establish their own limita-
tions and yours has set the figure at a seven percent maximum for
annual raises. Some employers instituted a salary "freeze," which
meant no increases at all; and more than a few have, for the first time
in decades, actually introduced salary *reductions* in 1982–1983. Despite a company's internal guidelines to department heads, there is a
certain leeway allowed for special or unusual situations. The boss
who wants to "stretch" the guidelines by giving someone a larger
increase than the seven percent base generally has to justify the move
with superiors or a compensation committee.

Your boss's 1983 offer to you stretched as high as twelve percent,
i.e., $3,000. Your request to match your associate requires an al-
most forty percent increase, *plus* whatever he gets this year. At this
point your boss said his hands were tied. He was not lying, nor

disparaging your work or your value to him and the company; the situation is simply out of control. You might project these two salary patterns for the coming four years. (All of this math is a cinch to do; just flick around on your trusty pocket calculator). Let's assume business improves and both you and your colleague get ten percent raises each year. Here's the future:

| | You | | Him |
|---|---|---|---|
| | | | |
| 1983 | $25,400 | | $34,650 |
| | + 2,540 | (10%) | + 3,465 |
| 1984 | 27,940 | | 38,115 |
| | + 2,794 | (10%) | + 3,812 |
| 1985 | 30,734 | | 41,927 |
| | + 3,073 | (10%) | + 4,193 |
| 1986 | 33,807 | | 46,120 |
| | + 3,381 | (10%) | + 4,611 |
| 1987 | $37,188 | | $50,731 |

As you can see, with the same percentage raises, you'll be making a bit over $37,000 in four years but he'll be hitting close to $51,000—a hefty $13,500 difference. Already, in the past three years, he's collected $12,650 in raises while yours amounted to $9,400—a dollar difference of $3,250. And don't forget: This projection assumes you are both rewarded *equally* for superior performance. By 1987, he'll have collected $28,731 in increases, compared to your $11,188. Look, Jane. See the wage gap. See that ole debbil, *percentage* increases.

All this happened because you didn't negotiate your starting salary, whereas your associate did. If you'd just bargained *a little bit* and gained $1,000 to $2,000, it might have reduced the pot available to him and narrowed the starting gap considerably. At this stage, your only solution may be a job change, moving to a company where you start at the salary you now know the job can command. But be careful not to make the same mistake again and jump at the first offer—it's bound to be at the low end of the spectrum again!

If you elect to stay with the company you love, you'll have to do some hard bargaining. Don't treat that first raise offer as final. Use that eight to twelve percent spread ("between $2,000 and $3,000") as the current guideline and negotiate in four percent increments. With persistence and fortitude, you might wangle twice that increase. After all, the arbitrary guidelines apply to the company's total payroll, not to an individual's annual raises. There must be *some* employees who don't deserve any raise at all; but that's the boss' problem, not yours.

Madeleine Swain, an associate with Eaton-Swain outplacement consultants in New York, deals exclusively with high-salaried professionals and executives. She meets women who are necessarily aggressive or assertive in most matters having to do with their careers. But when it comes to evaluating their starting salary, she says, "it's surprising how many don't even realize that this is a highly negotiable situation."

Here's a case where "not knowing" is a very expensive luxury.

## ASKING FOR RAISES

*Dear Betty Harragan:*

*Recently I quit my job as market editor of a midwestern trade magazine. While my friends toast my integrity for leaving an intolerable situation, I feel empty. I loved the job, the clout I wielded as a columnist, the local fame I achieved as an industry expert. When I accepted the position, the salary was not competitive with other job opportunities, but I was promised an increase at the beginning of the next fiscal year and figured the potential would offset what I viewed as an initial "training salary." The publisher reneged on his promise, and when I approached him to discuss my checks, he put me off with repeated evasions and vague innuendoes that he'd "talk to someone" about it. I later discovered this is his usual roundabout manner when dealing with salary negotiations. Meanwhile both he and my senior editors were complimenting me on my good work.*

*When I confronted him the fifth time and he said, "Well, you'll get
that raise in a month or so," I resigned, saying I could neither respect nor work for a person who could not keep his word. It was clear
I could not work under those appalling conditions, yet I miss the
position. How else could I have handled the situation?*

*Hollow*

Dear Hollow:

You have participated in a perfect no-win game. Nobody profited
as far as I can see. You are out of a job you liked; your immediate
boss is out an enthusiastic worker; the publisher must replace an
underpaid editor.

Could you have handled the situation better? I'd certainly like to
think so, since your outcome was sheer disaster. Even though I
don't know any of the live actors in this drama, common sense
dictates that there was unexplored room for negotiation because
only morons willingly play no-win games—and let's assume none
of you are that.

There are many clues in your letter that you did not understand
what was really going on. Like so many women approaching salary
discussions, you plunged ahead without any prior analysis of the
situation and without anticipating most of the conditions you might
encounter. By not plotting a strategy, including alternative approaches in case of resistance, you reveal that you don't grasp the
very essence of negotiation. Dealing with money in business is invariably a barter situation. That means you and your employer (the
boss) are engaged in a process of dickering over the price of a certain commodity. Your publisher is the buyer and you are the seller;
the commodity is your time, talent, expertise, etc.

The buyer wants to forge the best bargain he can, the seller
wants to get the best price possible for her services. This process is
known as salary negotiation but it has all the characteristics of a
strategic game such as tennis, chess or poker. That's why it's popu-
larly referred to (at least in male business circles) as a game—because the basic rules follow the pattern of real games. In other
words, there are some fundamental unwritten rules and requirements. For instance, no game ensues unless somebody starts one.
No game progresses unless the participants interact. It's a given in

games (and bargaining sessions) that when two or more persons are involved, their actions (or reactions) impinge on each other's decisions, which then trigger a response from the other party, and so on.

When a game disintegrates as yours did, it means that somewhere along the line, somebody—or both people—made serious miscalculations about how the other person would react. Your employer could be partly at fault if he never expected you to resign, inasmuch as you obviously enjoyed the job. Maybe he gambled that your psychic satisfactions overwhelmed the monetary rewards, so he could safely procrastinate in paying your increase. On the other hand, he has a pattern in salary negotiation that operates regardless of the individual involved—what you described as his "usual roundabout manner"—so he may simply have acted according to his norm and granted the seller (you) the first move.

Not knowing what was expected, you defaulted on the opening serve. You blithely assumed that an oral promise made during the hiring procedure would automatically be implemented on a certain date. Such an assumption is not realistic. It is naive to expect a busy superior to remember every passing comment he made to various employees months ago. Your raise was very important to you but not the least bit important to your boss. He had no motivation for remembering because he saved money every day he didn't pay it. Besides, he knew the first move was up to you, and until you made it, no salary game was under way.

You should have foreseen the possibility of his "forgetting" and started reminding him of the upcoming date weeks or months beforehand. If all this talk of game-playing is too formidable for you, think of it another way: You sold him a commodity (your services) with an agreement that he'd pay so much on one date and so much on a subsequent date. According to standard business practice, you then had a responsibility—*to send him a bill before the payment was due.* (Do you pay your phone bill before you get it?)

Having missed the first move, you were then thrown on the defensive and took the only action open to you at that point—protesting the lack of payment. For your boss, this was the opening salvo in the game, and he responded with his patterned technique: evasion and vagueness. There's nothing unusual about his methods;

dilatory tactics seem to be the classic Boss Response to wage discussions. The unfortunate part is that you were astonished by his actions. Apparently the behavioral information would have been available had you sought it out, since you later discovered that's how he always acted. But you were caught unawares because you hadn't done your homework, hadn't predicted how he might react or how you should respond in turn. It's as if you were standing immovable in the far court when he was known to always plop the first ball just over the net.

Your abrupt decision to quit was the wrong move at the wrong time. Despite the earlier stumbling, you two were finally engaged in a volley, actually discussing the timing of the raise. You failed to realize that this was the core issue, since he never seems to have disputed the promised amount. The fifth meeting provided your cue to start negotiating the date. (A skilled salary negotiator would have pressed even further and gone for a raise retroactive to the original date.) Instead of seizing the moment to win your point, you suddenly walked off the court in a self-righteous huff. Ergo, nobody won; everybody lost.

Quitting a job without another one in hand almost always signals a lack of game-playing skills. It's a no-win move. Worse yet, it removes you from the field of action and prevents you from learning or improving these essential techniques. Salary games must be initiated constantly throughout your job life. It's the only job skill at which you can never be too proficient.

You lost this game, but it doesn't sound like you lost much, since you were playing for very low stakes. The size of the stakes doesn't change the negotiating principles, of course, but each successive effort to raise your salary gives you a higher base to start from in subsequent negotiations.

On your next job offers, negotiate your starting salary to make sure you don't accept anything less than the high end of what you calculate as the "competitive rates" for your industry, location and experience. The starting salary is always the key negotiation. Subsequent raises (and cost-of-living allowances) are generally figured on a percentage basis, so a too-low starting salary means you fall steadily behind no matter how good your negotiating skills. It's a mathematical certainty (see pages 138-142).

P.S. Where does "integrity" come into this scenario? That's a tricky word (and concept). Negotiating a raise has nothing to do with moral principles; it is a simple matter of business necessity.

# YOUR INDUSTRY INFLUENCES SALARIES

*Dear Betty Harragan:*

*I'm a reporter on a newspaper in the suburbs of a major city. My colleagues and I are disgusted by the double standard attached to our jobs. We journalists carry heavy responsibility; we must get the facts, get them fast, and get them right. We are told, on many fronts, that we have enormous power and that we can make or break causes, people, and the paper itself. Yet we are not paid adequately for the important service we perform for the community. I want to be compensated for my four years of college, for the nights and weekends I must work, for the time I spend on research and reading to stretch my mind.*

*Last year my paper began cost-cutting when advertising revenues fell because of the recession. That meant letting some people go, instituting a hiring freeze and tightening up on supplies and expenses. We're so short-handed in the newsroom that we're not just busy, we're overworked—especially since three old-timers are recognized as deadwood. When I asked for a raise on my first anniversary, I had a list of twelve legitimate reasons why I deserved it. For two months before, I really broke my back to do a super job. I thought that then the editor just couldn't refuse me. What a joke! He wouldn't even hear me out. It seems I'd been given the measly seven percent doled out after six months' probation, so now he tells me I'm not eligible again until a year after that. Management's attitude is, "If you don't like it, leave." They know there are thousands of eager new graduates willing to swallow $12,000 a year to get into the business.*

*Many of us feel the owners don't care about their employees or they'd pay to keep a staff who works hard. As you can guess, I'm looking elsewhere for a job in journalism, preferably on a paper with a union (the last person who verbalized that word around here got* *canned even though everybody knew it was illegal). I'm fairly confident that two years' experience after graduation (here and at a previous paper) will allow me to leave this wage ghetto. Even $14,000 would keep me happy for a while, but how can you persevere in requesting a raise when your boss literally walks away from you?*

*Mad*

Dear Mad:

I only wish the thousands of eager young women flooding the journalism schools around the country could hear your tale of woe. It's depressing to read the collection of similar letters I've received from women editors and award-winning reporters who complain of underpayment, lack of recognition and dismal prospects. What's most dispiriting—from your point of view—is that several are long-term employees of the prestigious, unionized publications to which you aspire.

Bad news absolutely abounds in your chosen profession. You have put your finger on several crucial items, but you haven't yet incorporated them into an intelligible whole. You seem to be flailing randomly at assorted "villains" and getting progressively madder as your efforts to get a raise are thwarted. Your frustration is understandable, but it almost guarantees that pure perseverance in accosting your boss will not be successful. Your problems stem from more fundamental sources than you seem to grant. Unless you put all the elements into perspective, your anger will fester until your performance suffers and you become one of the canned instead of the canny.

The prime villain, in your mind, seems to be the company itself—the owners, management, editors and your boss. You sound as if all are conspiring to prevent you from getting the increase you "deserve" because you work hard. When your raise expectations didn't materialize, you jumped to the conclusion that "they don't care about employees," that they run a "wage ghetto," and that they practice a double standard by demanding high-quality performance while not reimbursing you for your college education. As a matter of fact, some employers are guilty of your accusations, but I'm not so sure your paper is one of them.

For instance, you mention two years' experience after graduation, which puts you in the class of 1980. In your central geographic area, the average starting salary reported by 1980 graduates of a well-known journalism school was $10,773. The average for those who started on daily papers was $11,271, while weekly papers paid $10,013 to beginners. Interestingly, you don't mention whether you work on a daily or weekly, or what the circulation is. Are you aware that newspaper salaries depend strongly on these two factors? It's entirely possible that you are paid above average for your experience and location, rather than being in a "wage ghetto." I would suggest that you write or call your alma mater to request a copy of the job survey that most schools compile for each graduating class. Find out what kinds of jobs and salaries your classmates got, so that you can judge better your own achievement to date.

Another factor that has significant impact on journalistic salaries is also absent from your report. You refer to "my colleagues" repeatedly but give no clue as to whether these are males or females. Once you put your investigative-reporter skills to work on newspaper salary statistics, you'll find that women's salaries invariably are lower than men's, illegal though that is under the Equal Pay Act. In the journalism-college survey I cited, the actual salaries for women graduates averaged $10,400, while men's averaged $11,170. That's a $770 annual difference to start with and, using an arbitrary seven percent increase a year, would make women's salaries after two years, $11,807, while men would be up to $12,790—a wage gap of $983. As long as increases are based on percentages, women's salaries fall steadily behind if they start off lower than men's. In other words, hard work and professional experience serve to lower women's wages in relation to men's if women continue to ignore the gender differentials that still are rampant.

Your next step, then, is to survey your current colleagues and see if you can find out how much they are paid and if there's a difference between men and women of comparable experience. That's not necessarily an easy task, but young people often are more willing to share salary data than older employees who were brought up to believe that talk about money is "not nice." Thank goodness, today's young people are apt to be more realistic and honest on this score. The trouble is that young women like to pretend that sex discrimination doesn't apply to them, and they shirk their responsibility to fight this pernicious practice. The union issue you mentioned illustrates this passive mind-set. Although "everybody knew it was illegal," the rest of you evidently sat back and watched a co-worker get fired for mentioning an issue that is of mutual concern to all of you.

Nevertheless, I agree that $12,000 is an abysmal salary for a college-trained professional of any gender. That's why I wish enrolled journalism majors (including you a couple of years ago) would start practicing their craft while in school and seriously investigate the occupation they plan to enter. It's never been a secret that journalism in its heydey was one of the lower-paid professions—in its waning years (as now), salaries can only go down. Famous big-city dailies (many highly unionized, by the way) are going out of existence at a terrifying pace. The market for journalists is shrinking rapidly, but the supply of college-trained beginners is proliferating just as rapidly. You are right to be frightened by the hordes of newcomers ready to pounce on your job. Industry estimates predict three to four new graduates for every job, but I suspect the situation may be worse than that. A young friend who graduated last year from a highly rated eastern journalism school told me that only five of her eighty classmates had been offered a job as of June 1982.

What these bleak projections tell you is that you're mad at the wrong people for the wrong reasons. Raise requests cannot be treated in a vacuum. First, one must ascertain whether there is any money to be had. When your boss turns his back on you, it's probably because your arguments aren't pertinent to the situation. But there's always one argument that commands attention. What if you offered to help the company make money, rather than spend it? Have you ever thought of switching to the business side of publishing, where there is not an oversupply of people, especially women? You said the crunch developed because ad revenues fell. What your paper needs is an eager young sales rep whose long hours and hard work will generate revenue. You might try to swing a deal using your present salary as a guaranteed base, plus commissions on what you produce in new advertising dollars.

That way, your efforts would pay off and you'd be launching yourself on the only lucrative career path in journalism—toward management—a goal rarely attainable through the editorial function.

## THE POLITICS OF EXPENSE ACCOUNTS

*Dear Betty Harragan:*

*I can't believe what I heard my boss say. He called me in for an appraisal after my first six months on the editorial staff of a prestigious national magazine. I expected to hear that I was doing splendidly since I've received many compliments and, Lord knows, I've worked like a demon—early and late, no lunch hours, etc.—to ensure a quality performance. Instead, he said he's wondering if I "have the right temperament for this position" because I'm not using my expense account! I watch the men around here and see them ripping off the company at every turn. Some eat out every day at fancy restaurants, or go to the theater at night and charge it off on their expense accounts. Unnecessary long lunches are a waste of time because I accomplish more by scheduling appointments in my office. I've been an editor on smaller publications where honesty and efficiency were applauded. It's crazy to think I might be fired for not cheating on the expense account. Did I hear him right?*

*Legitimate*

Dear Legitimate:

Yes, you heard right but you certainly didn't get the message. You should be thanking your lucky stars that you have such a decent boss; he's tipping you off that you haven't accepted some of the major responsibilities of your job. I suspect he's given you a few hints before, but you didn't pick them up, so now he's concerned about your business judgment.

Relax; he won't fire you just yet but he has reason to worry. Your lack of understanding about the role of money in a company's success sticks out all over. Just notice your attitude toward spending corporate funds: ripping off the company, inefficient, unnecessary waste, improper, dishonest, cheating. (Not exactly flattering to your employer's financial controls.) Apparently you have fallen into the trap of so many women who were brought up to be frugal and can be racked with guilt when it comes to making independent spending decisions. It's time for you to forget the childish platitudes you've absorbed; you have to analyze coldly what an expense account is for.

Distorted feelings about money, shared by all too many working women, are your first problem. Money is the lifeblood of every business organism. It circulates constantly through established veins and arteries to nourish and sustain a healthy corporation (and the whole economy, for that matter). Expenses are essential components of that flow. Technically, they are considered part of the necessary cost of doing business, and no organization exists without incurring them. As such, they are perfectly legal, so much so that expenses are deductible on corporate income taxes.

Not all employees, as I'm sure you know, have expense account responsibilities, but all employees do have reimbursement rights when they are sent out of the normal workplace to conduct their jobs (to a meeting, a convention, another plant or office). The company expects to reimburse them for all the ordinary expenses incurred along the way. No employee is expected to (or should) spend her personal money—which is fully taxed—on company supplies or expenses—which are tax deductible to the business.

You, like anybody else, are eligible for reimbursement if you are sent out of town, for instance, but beyond that you belong to a class of employees who control discretionary expenses. That category is determined by your specific occupation or assignment and is composed of people whose work requires them to have extensive dealings with outsiders, that is, nonemployees of the company. These outsiders include customers, suppliers, contractors, industry associates, the press, government agencies, community representatives or almost anybody whose services or good will are important to the specific employer. How well you handle your expense account can affect your prospects for promotion; higher executives are selected partly for their ability to make financial decisions that redound to the company's benefit.

Obviously, sales personnel and anyone whose job involves development of new income (which is a prime task of senior officers) have the closest to unlimited expense accounts. The guideline there is "spend as much as necessary," but the unspoken end of the sentence is: "to bring in the business." Sales volume can easily be equated with expenditures, but even that is not a simple tit-for-tat exchange. A beginner saleswoman had an experience similar to yours. She watched a male peer get assigned to better and better territories while she kept plugging along in her original district. She knew from the monthly reports that her production was usually higher than his and she also knew that he submitted "extravagant and unnecessary" expense accounts while she was honest and cautious. She complained about the discriminatory advancement, and the sales manager said, "He knows how to sell and you don't; I can tell from your expense accounts."

She didn't have the long-range perspective her company was looking for. Although she was successful at immediate sales, she was not out in the field getting to know people and building up relationships with potential new customers. She didn't understand that her open-ended expense account was a form of risk capital—a gambling stake, if you like—that she was supposed to "invest" for the company regardless of any immediate dollar return on her sales report. Her relatively penurious expense accounts told her boss that she was a good order-taker (and thus a valuable employee in her way), but her male co-worker had the instincts of a "sales" man (so he got the opportunity to expand his efforts).

Expense accounts, in short, reveal a lot about a new employee's grasp of business operations in general and the employer company's specific goals or purpose. It's entirely possible that none of the young salesman's "investment risks" panned out in actual customers, but his heavy socializing and entertaining showed that he had the right approach—nothing ventured, nothing gained.

You are not in direct sales, of course, so you have to figure out why an expense account is attached to editorial positions. One reason has to do with the nature of the occupation. You are in a so-called "creative" field, as are most writers whether in magazines, publishing, public relations, publicity, advertising, radio, television, or whatever. The tools needed to perform such jobs are ideas rather than machinery. Management recognizes that, and just as it supplies metal-working equipment for machinists or typewriters for secretaries, it also provides the wherewithal for "idea" generation— i.e., discretionary expense accounts for the creative worker to get out into the world seeing people, sensing trends, exchanging thoughts, exploring public attitudes or seeking information. Long business experience has taught successful companies that appropriate original ideas don't germinate in solitary confinement.

As your boss indicated, it takes a certain "temperament" or personality to fulfill this business requirement, and you aren't exhibiting it (admittedly you spend your days and half your nights closeted in your office). In effect, you are doing only half your job, and the least important half at that. There are thousands of English majors who can copy edit rough manuscripts, but what your boss wants from you is assurance that you can provide sound ideas for future issues and locate the best writers to turn them into manuscripts. In his eyes, you could be accused of "ripping off the company" because you accepted a salary with no intention of doing the job expected but rather sought to superimpose your own conception of what the job tasks should be. I know you didn't intend any such thing, but many bosses can't comprehend that women's inexperience in the upper reaches of business leads them to strange conclusions.

Take your assumption that practices of small specialized publishers could be transposed to a huge successful magazine. Common sense (translate that "experience" and "training") would tell most men that financial constraints mandate smaller expense volume for a struggling young company than for an established major one. Of course a woman who pared expenses to the bone would be applauded there. But that doesn't make frugality a moral "good," nor does the situation serve as an example to be followed; it merely reflects a specific business condition and, better yet, it leaves the bulk of the expense allotment for the publisher and a favored male assistant to spend! Using an expense account wisely *does* take considerable business judgment, so it's not surprising that the most common directive is, "Use your judgment."

In addition to collecting idea materials to perform their jobs, senior professionals and middle-level executives who mingle with the public perform a subtle function for their employer. They are perceived as ambassadors or representatives of the company and thus are tacitly charged with upholding the company's image or reputation. In highly competitive industries such as publishing there are accepted business manners or customs that build up over the years, and executive-level employees are expected to know what they are. It may indeed be wasteful, as you believe, to eat at fancy restaurants when a good luncheonette would do as well, but if your corporate guests are treated to expensive lunches by competitors, your shortsighted budgeting could backfire: The industry grapevine might soon be rife with rumors that your company is on the skids! Your company won't appreciate the image of being cheap, unmannerly or financially shaky.

When business is slipping—or times are bad, as they are now—the word may be passed around that "we have to hold down expenses for a while." That doesn't mean to cut down the quality of company entertaining, but it usually suggests reducing the frequency: Take someone to lunch three days a week instead of five, or postpone large-crowd events, or invite one key guest instead of three peripheral ones.

As should be clear by now, it is impossible to give any dollar-amount guidelines for expense account usage. Every case is different, and every woman has to figure out what makes sense in terms of her job, company, industry and economic conditions. Also, there is always the variable of your immediate boss's proclivities. Some bosses are penny pinchers and some are extremely tolerant. After all, many bosses—male and female—have no more business acumen than their inexperienced subordinates. Plus there's always the danger of the discriminatory double standard being invoked. It is well known (though never publicized) that women can be counted upon to scrimp and "save" on their expense accounts, so that gives more latitude to the high-spending males because the annual total of the departmental expense budget balances out. The possibility of the double standard is worth thinking about (and fighting against) if some boss starts nickel-and-diming you to death, but male peers have no such trouble.

The best guideline I can offer you is to pattern your expense account entertaining after male peers in the same job. If you ever get close to the top limit, your boss will undoubtedly have a few more gentle reminders for you. But maybe not, because by then you may have done such a good job you will have been promoted—and will have even larger discretionary expense responsibility.

# COMMON QUERIES ABOUT EXPENSE ACCOUNTS

*Can I take a friend to lunch?*

Of course. It's rare for anyone to do business with enemies. Presumably everyone you entertain is a friend or someone you're trying to cultivate as a friend. If you can project a direct or indirect business advantage, it makes sense. It might not be too sensible if the connection is remote and you did it every week.

*Can I charge off the fancy dress I have to buy to attend a formal affair at the company table?*

No. Professional executives are expected to own proper attire for business-oriented occasions. Such expenses come out of your salary unless you've arranged for a special clothing allowance as a business necessity.

*Can I get reimbursed for taxis when I work late?*

Yes. If your job requires that you stay at the office after dark, or if the neighborhood is lonely and isolated, don't take chances. Your personal safety is an asset to your employer and should be valued. Women are apt to get more leeway here than men, even to calling a chauffeured limo if the situation warrants. Occasionally the double standard works in women's favor.

*Can I include the beauty parlor when I get my hair done at conventions?*

That depends on the time away from home and your role at the convention. For short two- or three-day trips probably not, because you should have started in good shape. For an extended tour when you don't have access to your home facilities, yes. This is also true if you have a key public role and should look your very best at a specific time. Women may have to fight for this item because men don't usually need it and aren't used to seeing it.

*When I'm alone out of town, how much can I spend for my dinner?*

Whatever the best restaurant in the hotel costs—and don't order the cheapest thing on the menu. Any restaurant in an equivalent range is fine, and you can add a cocktail or wine onto the tab (unless your company forbids alcohol).

*Isn't it cheating to include wives in expense account entertainments?*

Not necessarily. If the business guest feels more comfortable (or wants his own wife along), the corporate host is almost obliged to accede to the request. In many companies, wives were traditionally looked upon as unpaid, silent employees, and even today some firms maintain a "family orientation" and approve of occasional inclusion of wives. The modern term is "spouse," and women executives should consider the advantages of inviting their husbands along when a necessary nighttime entertainment of a male customer might prove tricky or suspect.

*Do you need receipts for everything?*

No. The I.R.S. sets the limit at items over $25, but companies set their own rules on lesser amounts. There is no way to get receipts for coin telephones, newspapers, bus fares, short cab trips, airplane headsets, vending machines, tips, and similar cash outlays, but all are reimbursable on out-of-town trips. Keep accurate personal records of every cent you spend so you don't lose money, but you don't have to "prove" every nickel and dime on the expense account tally.

*Is it legitimate to charge off at-home entertaining?*

It's legitimate and widely done—by men. Women probably have to be more circumspect, especially if they're single and entertain men. In this case the double standard works against a woman, and her boss may question her "good judgment" in making such a decision. A party or group dinner, however, would be acceptable if her job and home circumstances made it appropriate. In any case, this is a once-in-a-while event, not a weekly or monthly routine.

*Who is considered a good business contact?*

It depends on your business. If you are a union representative, you would have to cultivate political people and their staffs, other lobbyists who might cooperate on your issues, key officials in your many locals, other union officials, the press, community leaders, workers in non-unionized shops, etc. The list is open-ended; the decision revolves on what you're trying to accomplish and who might have some impact on smoothing the path to that goal. A bank officer would have a different type of "contact"—for instance, business executives who control the disposition of a certain amount of funds, plus their friends and competitors who might alert you when a company is dissatisfied with its present banking connection. Someone in the fashion industry would have to keep up with designers, fashion magazine editors, fabric houses, retail buyers, model agencies, accessory manufacturers, commercial colorists, charity ball organizers—and one "keeps up" by taking such individuals to lunch, dinner, parties, affairs. This is the arena where business judgment comes into play, and that judgment reflects how well you grasp your employer's needs and your personal job responsibility effectuating those goals.

*How much "business" should be discussed at a business lunch?*

Maybe none. An outsider who surreptitiously taped a typical expense account lunch or dinner might be hard-put to decide if a single word of "business" came up during a conversation. Yet the casual discussion could have been immensely valuable to one or both participants. A great deal of significant information flows effortlessly from unstructured conversations. On the other hand, lunches or dinners can be all business: the parties exchange papers, finalize an agreement, make decisions, set deadlines, offer jobs, conclude any business deal more securely handled on a personal basis rather than through the mail or phone calls.

*How do I know if I have an expense account?*

You ask. The proper time to ask is during job interviews when you've reached the stage of discussing compensation. If your prior job included an expense account, assume the new one will, but ask how they handle expenses. Does the company provide advances or do they want things charged on credit cards and reimbursed later? Are there any per diem limits? Can you fly first class? Does the company have discount rates with hotel chains, car rental agencies, limousine services? Is there any restriction on how many clubs or professional societies you can join? Do you have access to company car pools or planes?

*Can I charge off lunches with individuals in other branches or departments of my company when I have to gain their cooperation?*

Not ordinarily. Employees of the same company are expected to work together without special inducements. However, if an outsider who falls in the category of a "contact" is present, then the expenses of the entire group (including two or more employees) are covered. There are other common exceptions, especially for department managers who welcome a new employee by taking a group of co-workers out for an introductory lunch. Bosses also have leeway under "administrative" expenses to take subordinates to lunch.

*Can I get reimbursed for attending professional conventions or career development conferences?*

Yes, but you often have to fight for it. As usual, your approach is influenced by your job. If you have an expense account, automatically submit the dues and meeting expenses for those organizations that have a business orientation of some kind. If you're questioned about the item, be ready to sell the benefits of belonging and attending. Be alert to the kinds of organizations men at your level belong to and argue for comparable treatment of your women's societies. If (as can happen) the company is adamantly against funding such meetings and lunches, simply sit with somebody who would be a legitimate "contact" and bill the expense as having lunch with so-and-so—don't mention the organization. If you think that's "cheating," you are not developing an astute business sense because getting around obstructive red tape is a prime managerial asset. Career development conferences are not, technically, expensable items; they come under different budgets. No matter what your job level, you should ask your boss how to get these paid by the company. Don't take the first "no" as an answer; be persistent and investigate ways to get such programs paid under personnel training budgets or tuition reimbursement policies. A small departmental budget may be limited but a big organization has many avenues to pursue—find them.

*What do I do when I see somebody cheating on their expense account?*

You damn well better be able to prove that you know what you're talking about. It is extremely difficult for an underling or an associate to make that judgment, and generally it's none of their business. The people who can spot "inappropriate use" of a discretionary expense account are those who approve the expenditures—managers, senior executives, controllers or chief financial officers. They see and keep track of all vouchers and any individual anomaly will stick out like the proverbial sore thumb. That still doesn't indicate cheating—there may be legitimate reasons for the most extravagant expenses. If you know that your boss's annual expense account is bigger than your salary, don't blame the expense account—start investigating why your contribution to this company's financial health is so severely underestimated and underpaid.

# CHAPTER EIGHT

# Sex Is
# a Business Problem

## SEXUAL HARASSMENT IN THE OFFICE

*Dear Betty Harragan:*

*I've heard about sexual harassment but I never thought I'd run into it. I work in a branch office of a national insurance company. Our office has the lowest turnover and the highest production record in the western division because our supervisor (a woman) is great; we work together as friends and have fun even during the busiest periods. The man who headed this branch was a fabulous boss, but we lost him a couple of months ago when he got a big promotion to the district office. His replacement is absolutely obnoxious. He screams at the supervisor, claiming she doesn't know how to manage, knows nothing about our state laws (I'm supervisor of policy compliance with state insurance regulations) and has violent temper tantrums. On top of everything, he is constantly pestering me for a date. I've told him no, that I never mix business with my private life, but now he is calling at night and on weekends threatening to come over. He lives in a motel since he was divorced just before his transfer. He's hinted that I might get the supervisor's job if I'm nice to him.*

*I hate him for ruining this nice job and destroying our good friendships. Besides, I live with a man and can't have this jerk calling me at home. I'm ready to quit. When I told my best friend my intentions, it slipped out that he's pestering me. She said he's been doing the same thing to her and she's also thinking of leaving. Is there anything we can do about this?*

*Very Upset*

Dear Upset:

Don't quit. That's what women have been doing for countless years but it's no solution; it's a cop-out. Sexual harassment on the job is so pervasive that women must face up to it and take the offensive. You've been lucky up to now because four out of five working women experience worse situations than you can even imagine. I've heard stories of $100,000-a-year men getting women executives alone in their offices, unzipping their flies and waving their penises at them. Or groups of men collaborating to alternately pinch, goose, flip the skirt, or make obscene remarks to a targeted woman co-worker. Most common is your situation, in which a male boss tries to wrest sexual or "companionship" favors from women subordinates.

What you (and all other working women) have to understand is that sexual intimidation has nothing to do with sex, attraction, love or any such romantic garbage. It is a power play. That's why it works only if the woman is vulnerable—a subordinate who wants or needs the job, a woman sales rep or entrepreneur who needs the business, a student who needs the marks or recommendation—or a dodo who thinks that's how you move ahead.

Still, high-level women managers have noticed that some male subordinates let it be known they wouldn't mind doing stud duty for their female boss! Apparently it will take generations to eliminate the male cultural conditioning, which implies that all women are susceptible to sexual control. But we are getting there. On November 10, 1980 the Equal Employment Opportunity Commission (E.E.O.C.) issued final guidelines on the specific subject of unwanted sexual advances, saying that conduct of a sexual nature, whether verbal or physical, is a violation of Title VII of the Civil Rights Act when it interferes with a woman's work performance or is used as a basis for employment decisions. It's high time this revolting practice be officially banned, but that doesn't help those who are caught in an immediate situation.

You've taken the first step in the right direction, however timidly: You told another woman. Don't stop there. Tell *all* the women in your office. You are apt to find others who, like you, are suffering this indignity in silence, too embarrassed to make it public. Unwelcome sexual attention from a boss is seldom due to your personal allure; it's a weapon used to coerce women. And I've been convinced for many years that the best defense against harassment is publicity and exposure of the tactic.

Don't forget your woman boss. Has it occurred to you that she is being disparaged because she was the first to reject his overtures? She is probably closer to his age than you and would be first in line to be "taken down a peg or two" since she obviously runs a successful back-office operation. When a high-performance woman is suddenly degraded, it's a clue to something fishy, especially since poor performance reviews are the common lot of women who repulse sexual advances. Whether or not she's married has no bearing on the situation. In fact, *if* she's married it strengthens the possibility that she is being intimidated in this case. Some men who are recently divorced, or in the process, may take out their bitterness and rage on innocent women co-workers. They may hate women at this stage, feeling that one just "took" them, and be ready to destroy almost any woman in their path who's in a weaker position than they are.

You and your co-workers have another advantage: a friend in the district office—your ex-boss. Get word to him somehow about what's going on. Do it unofficially if you can so that he can find an excuse to check into it with tolerable explanations at the regional level. You have to remember that so many men are involved in sexual peccadilloes that a well-intentioned male executive may hesitate to hit this issue head-on with his bosses. Meanwhile, you women are in a strong position, once you've coalesced around this issue, to reject further overtures by telling your boss to find his lady friends outside the office.

If any of you quit before the situation is resolved, by all means put the real reason on the final personnel exit form that goes to the head office: "Unwanted sexual overtures from Mr. X." This will never hurt you in future job hunts, and it will help other women by gradually unmasking those male bosses who intimidate women. It may also ensure that you'll get your unemployment insurance if you apply on the basis of "no work" or "company reorganization." What employer is going to refute your claim by saying, "Oh, no, she really quit because one of our executives kept making unlawful passes at her"?

## HARASSMENT IN THE PLANT

*Dear Betty Harragan:*

*I'm currently a "hard hatter" in the chemical division of a multinational corporation, and I'm disgusted. The few women scattered throughout this plant won't talk to me, and the men I work with have played every trick imaginable to discredit my work and make life miserable on the job. There's no help from supervisors because they're all men; complaints to the union (all male) end up with half-hearted, ineffectual attempts to stop the harassment. I've lost all respect for men on this job. They're mean. I'm not; they're devious, I'm not; they just don't act like decent human beings should act.*

*The women are not much better. They're passive and have no idea what games the men are playing. I tried to organize them into group discussions, just for moral support, but some of them leaked word to the men, who told them to treat me like the plague—which they now do. I sought help from outside women's groups, but they have no concept of what I'm going through. Why are we pushing for equal-employment laws when those of us who take the resulting jobs are shunned by women's support groups? Some of us are drowning in such positions without help.*

*I'm trying, though. I have plans for the future. In fact I've always thought I'd make a good chief executive officer. I'm good at what I do, and my background is good. I have years as an executive secretary (covering for inefficient, bumbling bosses) and two years of college. I will top out as a skilled craftsman in a month (I've threatened a lawsuit if I don't get it); then I'll finish school with a degree in industrial sales. Afterward I plan to transfer to our head office (although they don't know it yet). I'm willing to move or travel wherever the company sends me because my children are almost grown and I've lived all over the country.*

*I'm on the right track, but I need some suggestions. Where can I get financial assistance to finish school? And should I sue if harassment interferes with my craft rating?*

*Drowning*

Dear Drowning:

Don't give up! You are on an upward track, even though it is a highly innovative one for a woman. I hate to tell you this (we all cling to hope), but the unabashed hostility you're encountering is not unusual. In fact, it's par for the course when a woman infiltrates a previously all-male occupation.

Your trauma is intensified because you didn't anticipate the depths of resistance you'd stir up. No doubt you brought along many female white-collar illusions to the blue-collar world of work. Coming as you did from a ninety-nine percent female arena—secretarial work—you were unprepared for the ferocity with which men defend their segregated sectors of the work force. This is not solely a blue-collar phenomenon; it is a universal male reaction to invasion of their turf. Middle- and upper-level male managers fight just as bitterly to keep women out of their bailiwick, although they usually try more subtle tricks.

As a secretary, you didn't see that resistance clearly because you weren't in a position to compete head-on with white-collar males. But as a hard-hat you are confronting male peers directly. When you reach the stage of straightforward competition with men in management, you'll notice very little difference between a male colleague who hides your wrench and one who relays false information about a key meeting.

Your attempt to get support from other women was a sound idea, but perhaps you expected too much. Not all women are endlessly ambitious, particularly those new to nontraditional jobs. Unskilled blue-collar women often are extremely satisfied with the better-paying jobs they have finally attained, since these are big steps upward from the female service jobs to which they once were restricted. Understandably, they don't want to jeopardize their positions in a high-unemployment economy. In addition, you already enjoy higher status than they in the plant hierarchy—a skilled craft apprentice ranks above unskilled operatives or plant clericals.

It's too bad your female compatriots didn't realize the mutual benefit that could come from a support group, but some surely thought you "had it made" compared to them and couldn't see how they could help. Then, too, your description of them as "passive" probably is accurate, since they were easily intimidated by male bosses who ordered them to isolate you. In that respect they are not much different from a lot of women in every occupation: Women who have lived under male direction for their whole lives are scared to make independent judgments (what's surprising is how many *are* rejecting that straitjacket). Maybe you were pushing these particular women too far, too fast.

Clearly, you are not the most typical of ambitious women. The upward path you've chosen is so uncharacteristic that few women in craft, clerical, professional or managerial categories can even visualize it. That, incidentally, would explain why outside, non-plant women's groups could not relate to your problems. Their members would be predominantly white-collar workers who, unfortunately, are apt to draw a complete blank when it comes to craft or plant workers. Apparently you are one of the rare women who understands the vital distinction between "line" and "staff" jobs. The vast majority do not realize that line jobs are in those functions that *make* money for the company, while staff jobs are in those functions that *cost* the company money. One side is the profit ledger, the other the overhead-expense ledger (and chief executives always come up the ranks through the profit-making line operations).

In a manufacturing company, the profit centers are those operations responsible for making the products (the production department where you are currently located), and the sales functions (where you are preparing to transfer). Everything else is "staff," that is, support services for the production and sales line operations. Strangely enough, women M.B.A.s tend to spurn jobs in the production area even though major industrials still consider technical production background *plus* sales or marketing experience essential components in training future executives.

Most management men, of course, do not start out as skilled craftsmen, but for women this experience can be an invaluable door-opener. Who can say a woman is unqualified to be put in charge of a production operation if she was actually a member of the union "brotherhood" composed of those she'll be expected to supervise? Besides, such experience, as you're discovering, affords keen insight into predicting and deflecting male and female animosity toward a woman boss. Instead of worrying about suing your company over harassment, you might look on this period as tough education for later management prerequisites.

However, if you discover that unfair or unlawful methods are used to obstruct your skilled craft rating, be ready to take strong action. Work through the union, because unions are equally liable with employers for illegal discrimination. If your local does not adequately take up your case, go beyond it and fight for your cause through the national union office. If the situation gets sticky, you would be wise to consult a lawyer, but make sure the lawyer is an expert in *both* labor law and Title VII of the Civil Rights Act, especially in relation to sex discrimination.

When it comes to financial resources to finish your education, go through the company. A corporation the size of yours is bound to have formal tuition-refund policies, some of which may be targeted for women and minorities in low-level jobs. To play this game astutely, start by asking your immediate foreman and gradually go up through the chain of command. Intervening bosses may not know much about tuition programs, but in this way you are respecting their superior status while obliquely informing them of your intentions to move ahead in the company.

This process of inquiry will take you to the local personnel people; then, if they don't provide complete information, go to the headquarters personnel executive in charge of tuition programs. I hope you're not planning to quit your job to return to school. Don't—or you'll lose all the headway you've gained. Once you hit the mid-thirties age bracket (children almost grown?), you don't have any on-the-job training years left to forgo. What you can do is apply for a transfer to the industrial-sales department before you complete school. Sales jobs don't necessarily require college degrees; sales-*management* jobs do in this day and age, but by then you should be able to complete your degree requirements while still working at your job.

You've embarked on a most nontraditional path for future management, but in America's contemporary industrial upheaval you might find yourself bursting through on the fast track, headed straight for the top of the pyramid. Keep going and don't get discouraged during the rough periods.

If the harassment victims in the forgoing situations cannot solve their problems by going through internal procedures, they now have recourse to external legal remedies. Only in the last year or two has the murky fog surrounding sexual harassment on the job begun to lift. The first shaft of light appeared November 1980 when the Equal Employment Opportunity Commission (E.E.O.C.) issued final interpretive guidelines on this volatile subject. Aside from reaffirming that sexual harassment is a violation of Title VII of the Civil Rights Act of 1964, the guidelines clearly state that an employer (this includes employment agencies, apprenticeships and unions) "is responsible for its acts and those of its agents and supervisory employees with respect to sexual harassment regardless of whether the specific acts complained of were authorized or even forbidden by the employer."

Furthermore, the guidelines spell out conditions when conduct of a sexual nature is offensive: (1) when it affects employment decisions (salary, promotions, hiring, firing, etc.); (2) when it effectively interferes with an individual's work performance; (3) when it creates an intimidating, hostile or offensive working environment. Employers are warned that they have a duty to prevent such conduct from occurring: They must sensitize employees and managers to the issue; disapprove strongly of such behavior; set up appropriate grievance routes and sanctions for violators; inform employees of their right to protest unwholesome sex-laden atmospheres. Previously employers fell back on the classic excuse that "this sex stuff is not our concern, it's just a personal incident between two employees." Not, the guidelines make clear, if the offender is in a supervisory capacity. If the harasser is simply another employee, the employer is responsible if some company official knew of the conduct and failed to take corrective action.

On the heels of the final guidelines, much ongoing research on the prevalence of sexual intimidation began to surface. In May 1981 the U.S. Merit Systems Protection Board in Washington, DC, released its confidential survey of 20,000 federal government employees. The findings were appalling. An estimated 9,000 women reported they had been raped or sexually assaulted on the job; forty-two percent of all women working for the government (and fifteen percent of all men) said they'd experienced sexual harassment. The agency estimated that in a two-year period sexual intimidation had cost taxpayers $189 *million* in turnover, health care costs and lost productivity—thanks to widespread tacit acceptance of seductive work environments. The most discouraging fact in the findings was that only two to three percent of the 300,000 women victims took any official action against their aggressors. Most admitted they didn't know how to counteract harassment; they meekly quit or let themselves be fired. But note: Of those who fought for themselves, almost sixty percent won.

By early 1982 several other studies appeared. Two University of Michigan sociologists, Lars Bjorn and James Gruber, found that thirty-six percent of women factory workers in Detroit were victims of physical assaults, propositions, abusive language, verbal innuendo, or suggestive body motions. The researchers noted that sexual harassment was rare when only one or two women work in a department or, conversely, when women were a clear majority. The peak incidence of sexual abuse occurred when women made up sixteen to forty-five percent of the work group. A different study, by Wider Opportunities for Women (W.O.W.), a Washington, DC-based private organization, didn't find any distinctions for another blue-collar group—women in construction suffer a 100 percent harassment rate.

Back on the white-collar front, a sampling of 1,200 women in Los Angeles showed that secretaries and others in traditionally "female" jobs suffer sexual harassment because men look at them first as women, secondarily as business associates. But the U.C.L.A. professor, Barbara Gutek, who conducted this study had encouraging news. She found that where employers put sanctions on sexual harassment, men stop the behavior. Between 1978 and 1981 she noticed a great increase in men's awareness of the problem. If they might get fired or sent to therapy for making unsolicited sexual overtures to women co-workers they don't do it, she discovered.

Working Women's Institute, a New York-based national training center specializing in sexual harassment, maintains continuous records that confirm the enormity of this problem across all occupations, and its serious consequences for women of all ages and economic brackets. No job, workplace or job condition provides a woman with immunity; neither executive status, union membership, a "female" occupation, nor a family firm serves as a refuge.

The notion that sexual harassment could be easily halted if employers put their clout behind it doesn't appeal to a lot of up-and-coming management gamesmen. The reasons can be discerned in the incisive descriptions of this crowd by Michael Maccoby in *The Gamesman: The New Corporate Leader* (Simon and Shuster, 1976). A favorite technique to create an exciting, open atmosphere and to motivate male employees is to foster a sexy, gamy tone within the office. Maccoby describes how one manager expertly used flattery and exaggeration to titillate secretaries while "the men were encouraged to trade spicy, sexy repartee with the girls whc played a function that sometimes seemed a combination of *Playboy* bunny and housemother." None of these "girls," by the way, seemed to object; they adored this manager and willingly played along.

Of course, gamesmen of this ilk are not restricted to corporations; just as many are politicians. Less than a year after the harassment guidelines were issued, the Reagan administration gave vice-president George Bush a mandate to review thirty government regulations for the express purpose of eliminating those which were "burdensome, counterproductive and unnecessary." Guess what was high on the target list? Sure, those silly, onerous sexual harassment guidelines. Instant and furious objections from women's groups around the country managed to deflect the nefarious plan to abolish these vital legislative directives to employers, courts and lawyers. Thus, the laws prohibiting sex discrimination in employment are still intact, even though much of the enforcement machinery has been paralyzed under the Reagan administration. But the courts remain in place—so there's no reason for women to back down in battling for their right to work in peace, without having some slob treat them like the neighborhood prostitute.

# HOME ENTERTAINING

*Dear Betty Harragan:*

*I'm the only woman manager in the planning department of a highly ranked Forbes 500 company and would like your assistance in dealing with the de rigueur Boss-to-Dinner invitation. Does the subordinate initiate the cycle of visits to the home turf or is it more appropriate to wait until one has been invited to the boss's house? Can a single woman entertain her superior and his spouse at an informal supper or brunch in lieu of the formal weekend dinner? What should you wear for the occasion? A business suit is ridiculous (especially if you're doing the cooking), but how casual can you get without appearing sexy? Can personal friends be invited along with the business associate or does this not then qualify as a Boss-to-Dinner occasion? When a young woman boss has a young, unattached male subordinate, what's the best way to handle the situation? I've tried discussing these problems with friends my age (thirty), but their contributions usually consist of horror stories about fending off an eventual pass from the invited boss. Are there any new rules to go by for these unprecedented situations?*

*Bewildered*

Dear Bewildered:

I don't know if there are any "new" rules—or if any are needed—since the established "old" rules have withstood the test of time and provide sensible guidelines for women of all ages.

Your confusion in analyzing this problem starts at a basic level: You are asking the wrong questions. Your dominant concern, if you notice, is for the superficial detail—what to cook, how to serve, what to wear, who to invite. These issues are so minor in the larger context of business entertaining that executives have traditionally delegated them to somebody else. Guess who to? To wives. In other words, you are attempting to base profound business-political decisions on obsolete "female" social data. Inasmuch as you work in a corporate planning department, you would know better than most how the wrong data base can skew your results.

Women your age who were born in the 1950s naturally reflect the values you were taught or observed in your youth. Possibly you lived through a trauma that once beset suburban households on that once-in-a-lifetime occasion when father's boss (or some superior business official) was invited to dinner. (To a child, such a wing-ding could leave a lingering impression.) Even if you had no firsthand experience, you couldn't escape the "women's issues" of your youth, and high on that list (to judge by the endless advice spewed from women's magazines) was meeting the challenge of "entertaining" the boss and his wife. The isolated, bedeviled housewife of that decade presumably went into a tailspin of frenzy prior to the brief few hours when she was allowed a glimpse into her husband's big, important business world.

Moreover, the articles in women's magazines insinuated that the total responsibility for "impressing" the boss (and thus ensuring her husband's raise or promotion) devolved on the wife's handling of this dinner party supreme. Success in business, according to the popular media drivel of the fifties and early sixties, hinged on such abilities as folding napkins into tortured tulip shapes, making cute little faces on canapes or dutifully curling crispy red radishes. Little wonder that the wide-eyed female offspring of those years wound up with weird notions about business life.

The upshot of this upbringing is widely evident in the working environment of the 1980s. Women your age react to many ordinary business relationships as though they were the *wives* of the executives instead of the executives in their own right—i.e., focusing on less significant issues and bypassing the basic considerations. The crucial information that would become invaluable to forming sound business judgments in adult years hardly penetrated the home bastion and certainly din't reach girls' ears because their future responsibility was expected to be the same as mother's—limited to social duties, not to the initial business decisions. The various considerations that explained why and when it was appropriate to extend a home invitation to business superiors were not ingredients in the much-tested gourmet casserole.

Your letter reveals just such assumptions when you preface your questions with the "de rigueur Boss-to-Dinner invitation." Wherever did you get the notion that there is anything *de rigueur* about inviting your boss to dinner and cooking up a storm for him except from wild assumptions harking back to parental talk in your child-hood? Far from being obligatory, such an invitation is almost anathema! When over-eager, naive young men try that ploy, they are put down as unworldly; when overeager, naive young women try it, they are instantly tagged as "on the make." It's not surprising your friends report the invariable result as a sexual overture; they unwittingly set up a come-on situation.

Working is not and never will be a jolly substitute for social life. The behavior demanded of people within the confines of a rigid hierarchical structure is strictly disciplined. The guiding principles stem from rank-and-status authority relationships. Your boss is not your equal, no matter how friendly he (or she) is, and no matter how well you know the person from somewhere else. At work, especially in huge corporate bureaucracies like yours, the boss is ensconced as a distant, superior power figure—regardless of age, competence, gender, race or personality type. Misguided attempts to establish a personal, equal relationship are traditionally viewed by entrenched executives as deliberate efforts to undermine their authority. Some less experienced managers may not instantly per-ceive this status rule but they eventually catch on to the need for observing protocol.

Successful bosses rarely invite subordinates to their homes. On those few occasions when the boss does "entertain" subordinates, it is usually at a big party where the entire department is included—and when you accept the "honor," you'd better be careful because you will be under surveillance unlike any in the office. This may be masked as a social event, but it is a work situation; look upon it as voluntary (or involuntary) overtime. Incidentally, the same rule applies to company-sponsored affairs such as Christmas parties or summer picnics. More careers have been aborted by inappropriate behavior at Christmas parties than from inadequate performance on the job. These highly political "social" events are no place to get drunk, to "let your hair down," to allow intimacies from co-workers or to develop a loose lip.

Of course there are, in the normal course of events, times when you have a one-on-one engagement with a boss or subordinate. These are called business lunches and occur in well-patronized restaurants. The "entertaining" part is that the host (for example, a young single woman executive) selects the day, time, place and pays the check for her guest (for example, a young unattached male subordinate). The subordinate is neither expected nor allowed to reciprocate. This is not a social situation; it is an impersonal business association.

Since the beginning of the Industrial Revolution, working men and women have maintained their homes as a private refuge from workday pressures and interference. Today's ambitious young women are well advised to *keep it that way!* If you do, you may someday rise to those senior officer positions where more expansive considerations on home entertaining come into play.

## LOVE AND ROMANCE AT WORK

*Dear Betty Harragan:*

*I'm having a problem at work that I fear may turn into career disaster for me if I don't do something about it. I am in love with my boss's boss. I'm at a fairly high level in a fairly large (several thousand employees) conservative company. This man reports to the president and is in a very powerful position. I work with him, and he is my mentor. Six months ago I confessed to him that I was sexually attracted, and he admitted the same. Once at an office party where we were both drinking we wound up kissing and hugging (not seen by anyone). At work he's all business, but both of us are slightly uncomfortable with our sexual feelings toward each other. Twice I've come right out and asked him to go to bed with me, but he nervously said he'd made other plans. Any advice on the best way to add a bit of romance to the workplace—and, as I fully intend to do, to my bedroom?*

*Eager*

Dear Eager:

Have no fear that this situation may lead to career disaster. You have already blown your prospects at this company to smithereens.

For all intents and purposes you are now (or soon will be) unemployed, so let's see how you got to that stage in hopes you will not repeat the pattern. If you agree that a career path consists of maintaining a reasonable performance level in your current position, which ultimately leads to promotion to more responsible higher-level jobs, then you should also know that such developments require the support and at least tacit agreement of many other people you work with. No one can function alone in a hierarchy. Your irresponsible emotionalism has effectively isolated you from everyone—precisely what sentimental love affairs are supposed to do (and one reason they are so destructive for women).

First, you selected as your love object your boss's boss. How does that make your immediate boss feel? Just what a boss needs—some tail-wagging female subordinate jumping the chain of command to ingratiate herself with a powerful senior executive. Do you really expect this boss to be singing your praises as the ideal candidate for promotion? And what about continued professional performance at your present level? You admit the working relationship is already uncomfortable as you pressure the senior executive to consummate this fantasy affair. Whatever his faults (and they may be many), he is obviously pushing you away. Perhaps he sees the danger potential—a conservative company, you say?

You believe nobody observed your drunken hugging and kissing at the party, but I doubt that your unfettered emotional attraction to this executive is going unnoticed by the other female employees. I predict you will have a tough time ever convincing any of them that you have the judicial temperament suited to responsible positions. Your male co-workers also are probably watching this trash-novel enactment with deep suspicion. If anyone asks them to work closely with you in the future, most would decline the "honor," worried that you would try to jump into bed with any mutual boss to gain an unfair advantage over them. One or two might welcome the setup because they'd anticipate a handy bed partner, rather than a dependable business associate. So you can't win either way.

Then there's a newly powerful group you have antagonized. These are the serious career women who've been fighting to banish sexual harassment from the workplace. By far the most controversial directive issued by the E.E.O.C. (Equal Employment Opportunity Commission) is the ban against unwelcome, unwarranted sexual overtures initiated primarily by men and used to thwart the job progress of women. Many males (and their male management) were infuriated, claiming that they are not at fault but are merely responding to (or fighting off) female overtures toward them. Those men are referring to women like you—and as a result the sexual harassment guidelines stand in grave danger of being repealed. In other words, you—and women like you—can and will be blamed for using legitimate employment opportunity for sexual byplay, thereby jeopardizing the advancement of truly ambitious businesswomen.

It's unfortunate that there still are sexually innocent women like you, as well as those who indulge in sex with the cold-blooded intention of "getting ahead," or the lonely souls who fall for obvious phony male "lines," or the old-fashioned "girls" who are unabashedly husband-hunting in the job arena. Added together, they comprise a small percentage of today's working women, but their continuing existence reinforces the damning stereotype that says female human beings exist only from the neck down. What counts in wage-paying organizations is using your body from the neck up—known as "using your head."

None of this negates the undeniable reality that today's sex-integrated work environments are highly charged sexual atmospheres. It could hardly be otherwise, since everywhere you go and in everything you do, you bring along your biologic sexual self. Any situation where heterosexual members of opposite sexes are in constant proximity will be roiled with undercurrents of sexuality. But it does *not* follow that intelligent human beings in such environments will automatically start mating like cattle or dogs in a pen. Human beings are distinguished from the lower animals mainly because they do have mental control over their sexual instincts and behavior. Controlling an energy force does not mean shutting it off or denying it's there; it means holding it in check or, conversely, releasing it when circumstances are appropriate. The circumstances are never appropriate when both individuals work for the same company or organization unit.

As the workforce hopefully continues its march toward fully equal sex integration, I think we will see a growing taboo against corporate incest. In a way, such a proscription always existed, except that women were the only participants banished from the tribe for violating the stricture; men got away with it. There are a few signs that the double-standard is changing. I recently heard of a case where a company president got wind of a flagrant affair between two managers and called both to his office. He flatly told them, "One of you must go; decide between you which one it will be." Significantly, the man resigned knowing instantly that his future within that concern was dead. The woman stayed, but she too is dead from a career standpoint whether she knows it or not.

A fine romance, my friend, this is.

Approach this subject and you tumble into a hornet's nest of stinging abuse from die-hard defenders of everyone's right to indulge in office romances. In spite of the wishful thinking, trying to locate tenable examples of two employees who met, dated, conducted a romance and concluded the affair by marriage, cohabitation or dissolving the relationship—while occasioning no disruption in either of their careers at the same company—is so rare as to be the exception-proof. Such an uneventful idyll is nearly impossible if the two are collateral peers with advancement goals; successful liaisons are still generally contingent on the female being in a nonessential position and having no high aspirations.

What we have here is a contemporary can of worms, from which the lifelong career woman must extricate herself. By inveighing as I do against sexual entanglements with close business associates, I have been reprehended as inhuman, cold, brittle, unrealistic, hard-hearted, cruel and (most charitably) wrong. The upholders of love and romance in the workplace are both male and female, but their arguments are quite different. Men can be infuriated at the suggestion that their freedom to roam the work site in search of dates might be curtailed—by the women themselves, or more powerful men.

One young fellow who insisted he would "show interest toward any lady who appeals to me, be she secretary or corporate officer," is evidently running into roadblocks he attributes to me: "A fellow selects a potential date on the basis of who she is rather than where he knows her from. In this regard men are more liberal than women. Some women actually refuse to date men who live in the same singles complex that they do! A ridiculous restriction, yet your kind enhances this frightened attitude among the female population." Another man called me two-faced because I must know as well as he does that "women get these high jobs because they open their legs for the right guys on command"—and he can prove it with a couple of examples from his own company. So there.

Women critics of office chastity are more ethereal by far. "Falling in love is an irrational, incomprehensible thing." "Business logic is well and good in its place, but emotions know no logic." "We are all human beings who have not yet been able to decide with whom we will fall in love." There is a popular consensus that the workplace is the best place for single people to meet eligible partners: "People are able to really get to know each other and build rewarding relationships within this environment. Sometimes the relationship turns to love; sometimes to brief affairs." One woman asserted: "If all the people who were ever involved with someone they worked with were fired or stalemated in their careers, there wouldn't be too many successful working people around."

She's half right. There aren't sufficient numbers of successful working *women* around and one of the reasons is because too many careers have been severely hampered due to a love affair with a co-worker. The male partner rarely suffers career damage unless he proves very indiscreet—or fails to force the woman to leave after their affair is over! A woman who clearly sees the dangers in this double standard wrote to say she was "amazed that any woman in business would be so totally in the dark about such a fundamental issue of professionalism." Beyond that, she believes we should "give the lovelorn as little press as possible since attention to this drivel is a waste of everybody's time."

She's got a lot of company who share her opinion: perceptive, experienced executives who fully comprehend why sexual alliances with important business associates are proscribed. It's interesting to note that a recent survey of 400 atypically successful women interviewed by Nancy W. Collins for her illuminating book, *Professional Women and their Mentors* (Prentice Hall, Englewood Cliffs, NJ, 1983), uniformly answered "no" when asked if they condoned sex with mentors. At the same time, the author noted, this was the only question that almost 10 percent of the respondents chose not to answer; she speculates that the item was offensive or too personal for some. I suggest another possibility: They agree with my respondents who want this sex issue entombed for all time.

Much as I wish we could dispense with the practical realities of sexual attraction in a bias-free workplace, obviously that time has not yet come. Indeed, this is a *developing* problem that is rapidly spilling over into areas of official employer policy. The increasing prevalence of dual-career marriage partners, for instance, causes conflicts with those company policies that prohibit employment of spouses. Concerns about confidentiality of company secrets is leading some employers to look askance at employees who are married to or living with executives in competitive companies.

Sex won't go away as a business issue; it is first becoming a theme with monumental overtones for managements that previously relegated it to the category of unarticulated behavior rules. Intelligent solutions are not presently visible on the horizon, partly because people's attitudes about sexual activity are so contradictory. In addition, more and more young employees resent employers trying to dictate, or interfere with, their personal lives, providing they do their work satisfactorily while on the job. Nothing is more personal than who one dates or marries, so sex is on the front burner from every point of view. That's why women who are serious about their careers have to discuss it among themselves and assume some kind of leadership stance in recommending solutions. Otherwise, new sexual codes, written or unwritten, will issue from the same male management thinking that controls the current discriminatory standards.

For those women who sympathized deeply with the original advice-seeker in her pursuit of the man she loved, it may be necessary to explain why I was so hard on her. If she had been in a low-level clerical job or any dead-end position with little hope of moving upward or little interest in doing so, her urge to consummate a sexual alliance with a powerful executive (or anyone else) would be her private business and not to be censured. I am the first to agree that people have a right to fall in love with whomever they like and use every wile to go after that person—in or out of the workplace. Thus, I do not advocate a blanket prohibition against dating co-workers; to do so would be useless anyway because it goes on every place, every day.

My sole judgment on sexual activities centers on the role of sex in a business-behavior context. If a woman holds a position she wants to use as a stepping stone to a better position in that company or industry, her sexual activities are scrutinized more closely than her job performance.

Whether she's aware of it or not, in our society the sexual servicing of men is considered women's "business"—not managing departments, initiating projects, making significant decisions. At a juncture where these irrational perceptions clash, women have to weigh their options; either they subscribe to the traditional sex-object role, or they decide to pursue their nonsexual business career. As things now stand in our patriarchal culture, business and sex are inextricably tangled and women dare not ignore this reticulation if a satisfying career is at stake. Everything considered, it seems rather sensible to suggest that attractive women are perfectly capable of initiating a love life outside the retaliatory institution that pays their salary.

# CHAPTER NINE

# Painful Leavings

## RESIGNING WITH STYLE

*Dear Betty Harragan:*

*I need help on resigning from my job. Although I've switched companies a few times, always for a better position or salary or to get out of a frustrating situation, I've never felt confident about handling the resignation procedure. I don't quit until I've gotten another job but I always feel guilty about making the announcement. Usually I walk into my boss's office, explain that I'm leaving and hand in a short note giving at least two weeks' notice. If true, I might say I enjoyed working for the company, otherwise not. I never mention why I'm leaving and this drove my last boss into a rage. I think Personnel demanded he give them a reason. How could I tell them it was because he was inept, incompetent and a bully? Now I'm close to resigning my present job but, as usual, I'm nervous about the day I have to tell them I found a better position. I want to ensure a good reference if I ever need one in the future. Is there a sophisticated way to quit a job?*

*Timid*

Dear Timid:

Yes, there is definitely a technique to resigning gracefully. Judging by the lack of attention paid to this common career occurrence, you'd never know how important it is. There's a ton of counsel available on *getting* a job but practically nothing on *leaving* the job. Yet I strongly suspect that more women agonize over the formalities of quitting than like to admit it; they sense that there are threatening aspects for women in this situation.

Your letter revealed some of these undertones when you spoke of "feeling guilty" and "getting nervous." In addition, years after the incident, you vividly recalled a boss's anger when you quit. Evidently you dread duplication of that unpleasantness even though the personalities at your current company are bound to be different. Aren't you falling into the fatal fault of blaming yourself (i.e., your resignation letter) for a long-past childish tantrum by some dope? Chances are he'd have acted the same no matter how *you* managed things. Don't forget the distinct possibility that your quitting put him in a bad spot because you were doing the work you say he was incapable of handling so he actually was furious that you dared leave him in the lurch.

It's bad enough for ambitious women when old-fashioned male bosses expect competent female subordinates to do all their work without recompense or reward. But it is much worse when the woman absorbs that attitude herself and believes she has no right to better her job situation. That's usually the source of "feeling guilty" about leaving a job. Such inappropriate feelings get in the way of handling exit interviews intelligently.

Let's examine the realities involved in resigning. You are obviously moving steadily upward in your career by switching jobs when necessary. Since each change has been an improvement, new employers perceive you as capable and ready for added responsibilities. You have a perfect right to improve your job situation. *All* employees have that right—and men accord it to each other. A male boss may be envious when a male subordinate leaves for a better position, but he would never think of holding the other man back. Quite the contrary: He'd claim credit for having trained his subordinate so well! He might even exaggerate the importance of his co-worker's new job as if to advertise what great guys he has working for him.

Unfortunately, male bosses rarely accord female subordinates the same courtesy. Indeed, they often seem amazed that a woman on their staff could be highly prized by another employer. Consequently, the woman who resigns must play out this entire charade by herself. She must *overemphasize* the potential of her new job (even if she secretly knows its main advantage is getting her out of the place she's in). Thus, the technique for resigning is simply to explain that she's gotten this fabulous offer that she couldn't possibly refuse!

Personnel people are supposed to find out why employees quit, but that doesn't mean you tell them anything except the single acceptable reason—"a better offer." No one in business blames anyone for taking a better job; if you didn't take it, you'd be considered a dope. In future years (assuming the company gives out references at all), the only thing on your record will be: "left for a better position." And that covers everybody's ass.

Whatever you do, don't take quitting as an opportunity to spout off about crummy bosses, a lousy company, or unfriendly co-workers. Once you've decided to leave, turn into Sweet Sue and bemoan leaving this wonderful company but rave constantly about the great challenge your new job offers. Who knows? Someday this same company may try to hire you back, and if they make a good enough offer you may accept. After all, you'll have established the reputation of a comer—one who is always open to "a better offer."

Adverse reactions to this sensible, practical advice about resigning surprised me. The most bitter denunciations came from a group that apparently considers me their nemesis—personnel or employee relations specialists. Thanks to their complaints I am better able to see why frustrated, ill-used women who quit intolerable jobs are apt to make the common mistake of spilling their guts about bad conditions or abusive co-workers. I previously attributed this failing to women's desperate yearning for "things to get better" and their idealistic hopes that telling employers what's wrong would generate improvements.

Of course I did get some reaction along those lines: "If one takes your advice and does not tell the personnel people the real reasons for your changing jobs, the situation will never change. Is that right?" Some wanted more details on the timing and wording of the resignation letter because their primary concern is "leaving a good impression with their boss when they leave for a new job." A few sounded just plain vindictive and didn't like to be deprived of their final chance to vent their anger and "make trouble" for their recent boss.

These are normal emotional reactions (the very ones that need to be controlled), but I did not fully appreciate the pressures exerted by personnel employees who coerce departing women into these damaging outbursts. However, some of these employee relations experts indignantly chastised me for interfering in their bailiwick. These critics were representatives of major corporations and, naturally, in this classic female ghetto, were themselves women. One said:

> Job selection and training is costly and time consuming. I doubt her boss felt she should do her work without recompense or reward. I believe an employer is entitled to some explanation, a tactful one if you wish a recommendation later. To attribute ineptness to her boss may not be fair when the woman did not handle the situation properly. Your preoccupation with females in the business world clouds your advice. She should not handle the situation any differently than a man would. Let's try handling situations like this as professionals, not as men or women.

Exactly, my friend. Let's start with you as a "professional." You fail to notice that you immediately *blamed the woman* and exonerated her boss. If your job is to investigate employee problems, I'd have to conclude you are not well qualified for the job. Without referring to salary or promotion files, you automatically "doubt" that any boss (much less an incompetent bully) would expect her to work without deserved rewards. Aside from your blind prejudgment of who's right in this conflict, it further mystifies me how a woman could be honest with you about her reasons for escaping an impossible boss if she must simultaneously be "tactful" if she wishes a recommendation. Without realizing it, you have strengthened the wisdom of my original advice. The "tactful" reason is "for a better job"—precisely what ambitious men say.

An exit interviewer at a big oil company was even more confused as she expounded her opinion. She has the facts right but her interpretation of her duties is off-the-wall.

> Many companies have set up exit interview procedures in an effort to decrease turnover by alleviating difficulties whenever possible. The exit interviewer is an employee relations specialist who is not part of the resignee's work group. The intelligent executive should ask two questions prior to an exit interview: (1) What refer-

ences will be given to future employers? (2) What records are made of the interview and who may see them? In *most* cases companies only release dates of employment and title, so fear of bad references should not be a consideration. The second question is important. If only a few members of the personnel department have access to the files, then it is in the best interests of the employee and the company to be honest in the exit interview. The personnel department is generally the first screen in the rehiring process and if the interviewer feels she was given a fake or weak excuse, the individual may be labeled as restless or unstable and not reemployable.

Correct so far. But now listen to the rest of her letter:

If the individual was known to be a good worker and was frank in the exit interview, candidness will rarely, if ever, work against her. In fact, it may prove her to be ethical and concerned for the company's welfare. If the personnel department cannot find out what is wrong the problem cannot be corrected, everyone suffers, and turnover continues. My advice is to be honest in the exit interview. Couch your phrases politely, such as "I'm not bitter but I realize that you are interested in helping improve morale and job satisfaction so I'm telling you this for the person you hire behind me." The exit interview is an opportunity to help your co-workers, assist the company, and perhaps improve your rehireability. Most important, you will respect yourself and not feel guilty later for covering up your true reasons for going elsewhere. If a man felt an obligation to clear the air, he would do so.

I can't imagine what kind of personnel policy manual includes junk like that. It's laughable to envision an aspiring male executive on his way to a better job sitting down with an exit interviewer and engaging in so inane a conversation as "I'm not bitter but. . . ." Nor can I fantasize an upwardly mobile man agonizing about his "guilt" feelings because he didn't improve morale for his replacement by denouncing the boss! Astute executives (male or female) devote the exit interview to questions about transferring their medical benefits, insurance policies, pension and stock options.

For the enlightenment of those who don't have access to personnel files, here's the pertinent section of a widely used termination form. Generally this is all that's left of you after you've quit a company. Look over the blanks and decide for yourself which item you'd like checked— and which will probably put an X in the "yes" column for reemployment.

### Voluntary Termination

| | |
|---|---|
| Better Job | _____ |
| Family | _____ |
| General Dissatisfaction | _____ |
| Illness | _____ |
| Insufficient Pay | _____ |
| Relocation | _____ |
| Other | _____ |
| Unknown | _____ |

Recommended for Reemployment?
Yes_____ No_____

## TOO SOON TO QUIT?

*Dear Betty Harragan:*

*I was out of a job for six months this year because my employer was caught in the recession and was finally forced to liquidate the business. This had nothing to do with my performance, so I have excellent references, proven skills, and eight years of solid experience. I'd been on a lengthy job hunt and had turned up several promising opportunities. Unfortunately, the best companies kept putting me off or saying they were under a hiring freeze. Meanwhile, a company that I had serious doubts about kept pressuring me to take its offer on a "now or never" basis. Since I needed a job in this uncertain economy, I accepted, but the situation has turned out to be even worse than I feared. My problem is this: My first-choice company has now approached me with the news that it has gotten some exceptions to the hiring freeze, including the job I wanted. This is a big company, and the job seems like the ideal move for me at this point in my career, but I can't just up and quit my present job after less than two months! Everybody tells me I have to stay at least a year or my resume will make me look like a job hopper, or as if I got fired as fast as I was hired. The thought of staying in this awful place for a full year is getting me more depressed each day. Do you have any solution to this painful dilemma?*

*Torn*

Dear Torn:

Probably all job hunters, past and present, can sympathize with your conflict. Perhaps this predicament recurs so frequently because highly desirable job openings attract so many well-qualified applicants that distinctions are difficult for the employer; thus hiring decisions are unduly protracted. At the same time, less desirable employers are so happy to attract exceptionally qualified candidates that they try to grab them before the applicant gets a better offer.

As you point out, the stagnating economy exacerbates the situation. There is always a limit beyond which the unemployed cannot hold out, and I assume you'd reached that point after six months. If the recession showed signs of abating, you might have decided to chance it a bit longer, but under tight job-market conditions, further delay on your part could have been more of a reckless gamble than a reasonable risk.

In other words, I can see why your decision to accept an inferior job was a well-considered move under the circumstances. Who, after all, could accurately guess when another company would lift its hiring freeze? If you are berating yourself for taking this present job, forget it. You made a sensible decision, fully aware of the pros and cons, and you also weighed a crucial factor—the state of the business economy. Everything considered, you made a mature decision, not a rash one. There was always the possibility that this undesirable job, once you were employed, would turn out to be a more favorable position than you had anticipated. But apparently your doubts were justified, since the job is even worse than you suspected. That's not your fault. Admit that it's a lousy situation and you want out.

Follow up the reincarnated offer from your first-choice company as if a headhunter had appeared out of the blue. Inform the company that you're still interested but request a refresher interview. It's been a couple of months since you last investigated this job, so you want to make absolutely sure that it offers all the advantages you think it does. Specifically, make sure your responsibilities and the criteria for advancement are clearly understood by both parties. If the company has been under a hiring freeze and other cost-cutting procedures, you don't want to be surprised to discover that you'll be expected to do the work of three people or operate with an inadequate or nonexistent budget.

Actually, you are in a stronger negotiating position than before. The unemployed person is always vulnerable; even a poor job is better than none as far as giving you clearer perspective in evaluating a second offer. Whether you should mention anything about taking your current job is debatable. You'll have to use your instinct to decide whether such information will be taken well or ill by the new employer. Don't let your present employment interfere with your freedom to make appointments; simply take time off from the job you hate.

As you've surely gathered, I don't subscribe to your unexamined statement that you can't "up and quit" a job in two months. Why not? One of your own reasons was because your record would look as if you'd "been fired as fast as you were hired." You unconsciously verbalized one of the unspoken dangers: that an employer can (and often does) sever a job relationship very fast if the hiree is viewed as a mistake. Using the same argument, the employee can make the identical decision if the job doesn't turn out as promised. (Don't let your private doubts about the job obfuscate your thinking here—a hiring "mistake" is always the employers' fault. They have access to all the facts plus the opportunity to make comparative judgments among applicants.)

As to your other fear—that you'll look like a job hopper and that will leave a negative impression on your record—I'd say your worries are obsolete. Just read the daily business news pages and you'll notice that many senior executives aren't holding jobs for very long. Companies all over the country are cleaning house, reorganizing, centralizing, decentralizing, cutting staff, terminating loyal old-timers, hiring new people with different experience. Employees are inadvertently thrown into the job market as companies collapse. This is no time to be worried about job hopping—it's a time to be grateful that your skills are in demand in a convulsive labor market.

Concern about your future resume is also premature. One reason I recommend that you analyze your first-choice job carefully is to ensure that you'll have a significant tenure at the company you really like. As time passes, you'll merely eliminate any mention of this temporary stint at the wrong company, as if it never occurred. Two months, in the long run, is insignificant; it hardly matters whether you spent six months or eight months looking for a suitable position. In so short a time span, you've hardly become indispensable to your present employer, so the only problem you leave behind is a replacement for yourself. Don't worry; this company should have a healthy list of applicants who are waiting in the unemployment lines for *this* employer to make them an offer.

Quit, take the better job, and make both you and your replacement happy.


## ABANDONING THE FAMILY FIRM

*Dear Betty Harragan:*

*I am the sales manager of a small manufacturing company with twenty employees and just under $1 million in sales. I had worked for the company on and off until I returned permanently, six years ago, with the intention of getting involved in day-to-day operations. The firm is making money but has numerous problems. We have a woman financial officer who worked her way into that position over the years. I've begun to observe questionable practices in the financial area, especially with regard to the privately held stock ownership. Here's the kicker: The company was started by my father (who invented the product). He is now seventy years old and has pulled away from active management, although he won't retire. My father has made no plans for succession, and the financial officer is his girl friend. The company's future is uncertain, and as a result, so is* *mine. I'm seriously questioning whether it's worthwhile to continue in this situation. Do you have any advice that might help me make a decision?*

*Hopeful*

Dear Hopeful:

This issue is just coming to light as a perplexing problem for a growing number of contemporary women: Should an ambitious young woman continue working in her father's business, which, ostensibly, she might someday run? Or are internal frictions likely to stymie a daughter-executive trying to gain management experience?

Almost all the cases familiar to me have certain features in common. All are small, privately held industrial manufacturers with sales of less than $1 million. The number of employees ranges from 20 to 100, many of whom have been with the company since its inception some thirty to thirty-five years earlier. The owner-founders are now in their late sixties or seventies, yet none has made plans for the firm's future by acknowledging a successor. The final common feature is startling—all the companies have a behind-the-scenes power broker in the person of a long-term "girl friend" of the owner-chief executive. (Whether or not the owner has a wife doesn't seem to matter.)

Admittedly, mine is an infinitesimal sample, considering the 13.1 million small businesses in the U.S. (defined as those with sales under $1.85 million and fewer than 500 employees). Yet the existence of business-trained daughters trying to infiltrate their father's establishments by working up through lower-level management functions is a phenomenon of the last decade. In prior years, daughters might have been given a minor clerical job until they got married, but only sons were customarily "taken into the business" with the expectation that they would someday own and run it. Evidently, many sons are opting for separate careers in other fields, while aggressive daughters are now looking at the family business as a logical route to chief-executive status.

I automatically assumed that a successful father would feel flattered and gratified if his daughter expressed deep interest in his company, wanted to be part of its operation and to contribute her know-how and talents to its growth. However, that's not what my confidantes report. Without exception they say their fathers more or less "throw them to the wolves" and in no way support them or give them the benefit of personal advice; these fathers are the furthest thing from mentors. This puts the daughters in the unenviable position of facing hostile confrontations with older men who have been with the company for many years. In one case, it put the daughter up against some young men who were M.B.A.s, like herself, and saw a booming small organization with an aging C.E.O. as an unparalleled opportunity to reach top management quickly. (It appears that Hugh Hefner, who carefully groomed his daughter, Christie Hefner, to become president of Playboy Enterprises, may be a model businessman-father.)

Not knowing any of the executive fathers in these cases, I can't hazard a guess as to the influence exerted by the girl friend-employee. From what the daughters tell me, these women generally start with the company as either a bookkeeper or a secretary. As the business grows, they take over confidential financial affairs and develop intimate personal relationships with the boss. Unquestionably, they know more about the business's operations and profits than anyone—including family members—and participate in top-level decisions such as hiring and firing. They appear to be entrenched obstacles that no one, daughter especially, can get around. (Obviously, I did not get complimentary descriptions of the girl friends, but for all we know, *their* brains and business acumen, not the titular owner's, may be responsible for the company's success.)

Given this brief background, I'd say your decision depends largely on the personality of your father and your relationship with him. This, of course, is the main difference between small companies and big corporations; closely held owner-founder firms reward personality ties more often than objective merit, whereas the publicly held, impersonal corporations reward winners of the political-performance games that go on within the hierarchy. So if your future advancement depends on your father's closeness to you, that relationship becomes your primary consideration.

Clearly, your father has not welcomed your participation enough to indicate that you are a serious contender for the top executive spot. You don't even know if you will inherit a majority ownership when he dies. If you were sure of that, you could put up with a lot of flak in the intervening years and chalk it up to necessary experience that will prepare you for chief-executive decisions. Lacking that information, you could be letting yourself in for needless suffering, because the old-timers will probably fight you tooth and nail whenever you try to institute new methods or introduce different ways of handling things. In a family-owned business, it's very hard to gain respect and obedience from subordinates unless you have the benediction of the "Big Boss."

To make an intelligent decision, you really must get some clue as to the future disposition of the company's stock. If you are somehow closed out from a majority holding, you could be wasting valuable working years because "working for your family" is not considered the highest-quality managerial experience when transferring to another company, and you could slide downward in both salary and responsibility.

On the other hand, if you move out now and take a sales or managerial position in a related field and build an independent career, you will be accumulating training that would allow you to move back to the family business with a broader perspective—if and when the opportunity occurred. I'm not recommending that you move out. I'm strongly suggesting that you take a hard, analytic look at the personal entanglements that have enmeshed your father's employees and decide whether you have sufficient influence with him to control those personalities.

## BATTLING BAD REFERENCES

*Dear Betty Harragan:*
*Can you refer me to a woman lawyer who understands defamation suits? Two and a half years ago I lost out on a high-paying job in employee communications because a boss who had fired me gave a bad reference. The headhunter told me that the prospective employer, a suburban corporation, called my previous boss and asked*

*him if I got along well with executives. He said, "No." I was so
shattered I didn't do anything at the time. Don't these tough-
minded bosses know they can't just fire people and then destroy a
person's whole life with such lies? Meanwhile, I trusted the glowing
promises of the founder of a new regional publication. It has just
folded, and now I'm looking for a job again. This time I intend to
be prepared for the illegal, damaging statements of ex-bosses. I admit I never liked the idea of "playing the game" but I'm afraid my
principles will have to go by the wayside. I've always prided myself
on being a maverick, an independent thinker, but if I have to, I'll
get as tough as they are.*

*Ethical*

Dear Ethical:

Like many women, you have managed to thoroughly distort the
"game-playing" aspect of business. You instantly assume there is
something mean, despicable and illegal about it. At the same time,
you have an inflated opinion of your own "principles," which you
unquestioningly presume to be far superior to those of your various
employers. Such a combination of viewpoints will inevitably bring
you into conflict with bosses. From the overall tone of your letter I
can easily see how you'd have great difficulty relating to experienced executives; apparently you disapprove of everything they
stand for.

Let's examine some of your statements and implied accusations.
Your intention to be prepared is admirable. Indeed, that may be
the single legitimate requirement of game playing that you exhibit;
alert gamesters try to be prepared for any eventuality. Unfortunately, you are loading your cannon back-end-to. You anticipate
that ex-employers will vilify you with the same "lies" they used
before, while you admit that you deliberately don't get along with
superiors because, by your definition, they are unprincipled. Better
for you to admit your weaknesses and seek a job that does not
require constant interaction with departmental executives or interpretation of corporate policies, as employee communications does.

There is nothing illegal in a prospective employer trying to get a
tip-off on a job candidate. In suburban environments it is likely
that executives know their counterparts in other firms and use

friendship for off-the-record information, beyond official company references. That appears to be your downfall since your work is not in question, just your unrealistic attitude. For example, bosses *can* fire people; in many cases they *must* fire people. Most of them hate that responsibility more than any other (they know it's devastating to the terminated individual), but often there is no alternative. Certainly that's the case with your recent employer, whom you seem to blame because his new venture went bankrupt—as if he failed just to spite you and put you out of a job!

Frankly, I'm searching here for some clue as to what those high "principles" you espouse actually entail. What I sense is an underlying antagonism toward business in general, and a refusal to sympathize with bosses and to recognize that they have problems, too. I also notice a deep undercurrent of passivity in your complaints. Whatever happens to you is somebody else's fault; you had nothing to do with it. You operate, as you say, on a rarefied ethical plane, far above the mundane level of wicked games. Could that be a rationalization for avoiding action? An excuse for abdicating responsibility? Are you possibly using ethics as a screen for ignorance?

You see, the business game you reject is based on *action*. Everyone who accepts a paid job tacitly announces that she is prepared to play on a certain team or wants to sit down at a specified card table. It is assumed by everyone else that she will abide by that game's rules. Just accepting a job puts you in the game, like it or not. If you subsequently refuse to play, that is tantamount to coming to bat in a baseball game and suddenly insisting: "I'm not going to swing that silly wooden stick! I brought my own tennis racket from home and I'll only hit with that."

By some weird twist of logic, that might be called "independent thinking." It's maverick behavior, true. But what's to be proud of?

Nevertheless, your question about defamation suits is well-taken and deserves amplification. There is a growing awareness of employee rights and it's important to know the legal remedies available to individuals whose rights have been violated. A large body of the restrictions on employers evolved from antidiscrimination laws, which, among other things, make it illegal to ask job candidates their age, sex, race, religion, place of birth, marital status, housing arrangements, arrest record, type of military discharge, illness history, family plans or, in the case of women, any questions not routinely asked of male candidates. (Many of these questions are perfectly legal for tax or insurance purposes *after* the applicant has been hired.)

Possibly sparked by discrimination lawsuits, employees have become more litigious in general in recent years, especially with regard to information released by previous employers in response to reference checks. The resulting court cases charging companies with libel, slander, invasion of privacy or defamation of character (accompanied by hefty damage claims) have had a revolutionary impact on personnel policies. Many big companies, to guard against these disruptive and expensive lawsuits, have decided to offer *no* information to reference-seekers beyond affirmation of the dates that the person worked there. Others are a bit more generous and give out the job title or positions held, although many demand a written request before supplying any information.

What this means is that women can dismiss their inordinate fears of "getting bad references," which frequently impelled them to put up with outrageous working conditions. As a general rule, the free-wheeling days are gone forever when companies can hand out reckless opinions, intimate details or character appraisals about ex-employees. Naturally this creates a problem for would-be new employers who are trying to verify the performance and credentials of candidates. There is nothing illegal about doing that, *provided* the questions have a direct, bona fide relevance to the specific job duties. In your case, the prospective employee communications job necessitated harmonious working relationships with assorted corporate executives (such jobs normally do), so the question to your previous boss was clearly job-significant and thus legitimate to ask and answer.

If the answer was a lie—and you can prove it—then you might have grounds for a slander suit. But we know there was one executive you didn't get along with—the one who fired you and answered "No" (which was true from his point of view). In other words, slander, libel and defamation charges are complex legal technicalities and require substantial proof. These are important legal tools to protect employees from malicious, abusive, hostile or prejudiced supervisors and managers, but they are not a cover-up for inadequate performance or "maverick" conduct on the job.

If, in your current job search, you look for positions that emphasize your strong points, there should be no reason for prospective employers to check up on irrelevant weaknesses, and your references could be positive this time. Don't blandly assume you'll run into a reprise of the situation of several years ago. Nevertheless, if you discover that ex-employers are *volunteering* unnecessary, damaging information, perhaps you should consult a lawyer. After all, these kinds of cases wouldn't be proliferating if there weren't a lot of unenlightened employers violating ex-employees' rights.


# THE JOB-SEARCH MEAT GRINDER

*Dear Betty Harragan:*
  *Six months ago I was a mature, confident, capable executive. Today I am a lowly clerical "temp." I've been ripped off, ignored or insulted by career counselors, employment agencies and headhunters. I was (am?) an experienced general manager for nonprofit artistic organizations—I handled budgets up to half a million dollars, hired and fired, supervised up to 200 people, did basic publicity and fund raising. When my employer ceased operation, I decided my administrative talents were transferable to private industry. First, I went to a career-counseling outfit that claimed a track record in transferring skills. All I got for my $2,000 were ridiculous suggestions from incompetent men, such as reprinting my resume in an expensive format. I tried to register with executive recruiters but they were obnoxious. All refused to see me except one woman who agreed to an hour interview for a $50 consulting fee. I exhausted the "hidden job market" by arranging more than fifty private appointments with assorted executives. Some were courteous and referred me to others, while some were downright abusive. None of these efforts provided a nibble on a real job. Employment agencies are hopeless. All they care about is my typing speed or sending me out on jobs paying $10,000—exactly half what I earned. Is there any way to stop this exploitation of women job hunters?*
                                                      *Demoralized*

Dear Demoralized:

I wish I could prescribe a miracle drug to ease your pain. Few stories are more heartbreaking than those of women professionals who inadvertently end up in the job-search meat grinder. The situation is debilitating to everyone, which accounts for the endless stream of how-to placebos, many of which you apparently swallowed.

I have no magic formula, but perhaps you can bolster your eroded self-confidence by taking a more realistic view of the process and people involved with job placement. There is nothing wrong with your goal of transferring skills. However, you are not paying attention to the economy. The news is replete with dire accounts of hiring freezes, staff reductions and budget cuts. A switch from nonprofit to profit sectors, difficult at best, is particularly uphill in a shrinking employment market. Given the circumstances, six months is not a long time to accomplish your purpose. Why are you giving up so soon?

You made a bad mistake by falling for the advertising come-on of a commercial "career counselor." I don't mean to rub it in, but if other women can learn from your expensive error it may ease your pain. These self-styled "job counselors" have nothing to do with placement. They are in the business of selling their services regardless of how inane, shoddy—or worthwhile—to gullible souls. What landed you in this trap was naiveté about the legal contract you voluntarily signed. Had you read the fine print, you would have known precisely what you were buying and would have realized that your investment had no connection to getting a job. The fundamental maxim for avoiding rip-offs is simple: *Never, never pay anybody to get you a job.*

You also sound muddled about the role of legitimate employment agencies and executive search firms. Linda Kline, president of Kline-McKay, Inc., an executive search firm in New York City, says most women share your confusion: "They seem to think that search firms should be helping the job seeker, whereas the opposite is true; search firms work solely for their business clients, which are generally major corporations."

In other words, headhunters are neither rude nor obnoxious when they refuse to see you; talking to job seekers is not their business. (If they do it, they have a right to charge a fee for their time and expertise.) Furthermore, headhunters (as executive search firms hate to be called) identify "executives" according to the standard criterion—salary level. Nowadays the minimum falls in the $40,000 to $45,000 range. Outside of their primary concern to obtain assignments from clients, the stock-in-trade of search firms is a huge, computerized dossier of up-and-coming executives whom they identify from myriad business sources, including personal recommendations.

The best way to get on a headhunter's list is to become well known in your field. All of them are deluged with resumes, but they will not respond to yours unless, and until, they are hired to find someone with your exact qualifications. Ambitious women in the appropriate salary range should certainly send updated resumes to search firms on a regular basis, but don't depend on them to get you a job when *you* need it; their timetable is dictated by clients. Incidentally, a search assignment can take anywhere from three months to three years so, from both sides of the fence, placement is seldom quick.

Employment agencies—unlike headhunters—are licensed and regulated in practically every state. This is intended to protect the applicants from unscrupulous operators because agencies do not work for job seekers either; they work for themselves. Essentially what they sell is time. More precisely, they save time for employers. Any organization can hire directly by placing an ad, then screening applicants—and most do for low-level, high-turnover jobs. If the supply of applicants is great for any position, companies don't have to pay agencies to find people. That's when agencies can demand that the applicant pay the legally fixed percentage of salary after she has the job. If you run into an agency that won't let you talk to anyone until you've signed its contract or "application," be wary. Don't sign anything that obliges you to pay! You can get that kind of job for free by going to company personnel departments.

Always look for "fee paid" positions through employment agencies but remember that their commodity is "warm bodies." Agency help-wanted ads are designed to attract as many applicants as possible, qualified or not, on the assumption that one ad will draw enough people to fill several job openings—and as quickly as possible. Some employment agencies are more specific. These focus on certain occupations or professions, such as engineering, law, accounting, teaching, modeling, nursing, copywriting. These can— and often do—handle fee-paid jobs at salaries that range into the high $60,000s and $70,000s. Not all the money is in the "management" occupations where the headhunters concentrate.

As for "temping"—don't knock it. There's no better way to gain a feel for the profit-oriented milieu of private industries. A temporary employer could be sufficiently impressed to offer you the permanent position you are seeking. It has happened to many others.

Any column that peripherally mentions job hunting produces a flood of requests for help. The pleas range from "How can I look for jobs while working when I commute from 6:20 A.M. to 6:40 P.M. and I can't call from the office?" to "How can I get a job in private industry when my background is all in government . . . social work . . . nonprofit . . . mental health . . . teaching?"

As deeply as I sympathize with the anguish of the job-searcher or career-changer (very few of us have not plumbed the depths of that personal horror), I do not rank myself as an expert in that arena. The kaleidoscope of job hunting is forever changing, while individuals have very different needs depending on their proclivities, abilities, experience and ambition. To be truly helpful and authoritative in this field demands full-time attention to that subject alone. There is somebody devoting the required diligence—Richard Nelson Bolles, author of the perennial best-seller, *What Color Is Your Parachute?* published by Ten Speed Press. This well-written manual is updated each year and is unquestionably the basic reference for a serious job hunter. Whether or not you adopt all the suggested techniques, the information is accurate and incisive. Bolles also includes a thorough, up-to-date bibliography of supportive resources, such as an excellent list of books by other authors, job counseling services and answers to common questions (especially those I encounter most often). I gratefully defer to him as the preeminent connoisseur of the job hunting market.

My realm of expertise starts after you get a job. In the last ten years more women than ever before have found jobs but then a host of new problems crop up, specifically, how to survive in those jobs and utilize them as natural stepping stones to more responsible, remunerative positions. My overriding ambition is to help women avoid the job-search meat grinder, even though that's not always possible in an economy as volatile as the 1980s has been and will continue to be.

Nevertheless, it is a goal worth pursuing because many of women's job barriers are independent of the state of the union. As myriad examples in this book show, most of the potentially damaging mistakes women make on the job could have been foreseen and side-stepped or can be rectified. You don't have to win every skirmish to win a war. Nor must you amass a perfect record in coping with every minor difficulty to build a successful career. Just know the difference between major and minor issues and be ready to launch a counteroffensive when somebody threatens to trample all over you.

There *are* unwritten rules you must understand and accept, just as there are strategies and tactics that will ensure your getting ahead. But when all is said and done, you are basically dealing with people—and that, my correspondents assure me, is what they want to do most as part of their jobs. In that case, you have endless opportunities to rely on your judgment, intuition and common sense when confronted with work problems that are new in your experience. Don't discard your female instincts, charm, sensitivity, manners, humor or personality. You are not out to transform yourself into a male stereotype—you are out to match men and beat them at their own game of economic independence.

# INDEX

accounting careers, 78–83
age, as factor in career planning,
    95–96, 125–127
ambitions, job-related constraints
    and, 113
American Civil Liberties Union,
    59
anger, as useful, 71–74
authority principle, 9, 17–21
    accepting boss's role in, 18,
        192–195
    accepting responsibility in, 27,
        32–33
    division-of-duties and, 19–20
    insubordination in, 20
    job description vs., 14
    subordinates' freedom vs., 13

bachelor's degrees, 131–134
banking careers, 54–63, 110–113
Bertin, Joan, 59
"Beyond ERA," 75
blue-collar industries, female
    white-collar illusions in,
    164–167
Bolles, Richard Nelson, 198
bosses, 17–43
    aggressive senior managers as,
        28–31
    career mobility and "duels"
        with, 15–16, 33–36,
        142–146
    conflicts between, 37–39
    criticism by, 22–25
    excessive turnover of, 110–112
    hostility of subordinates toward,
        25–27, 99–102
    incompetent, 31–33, 180–182

    open discussion with, 27,
        37–39, 85, 118–119
    overdependence on, 21, 32–33
    protective role of, 23–25,
        107–108
    rights of, to assign duties, 14,
        19–21
    subordinates' personality con-
        flicts and, 46–49
    sympathy needed for, 192–195
    women as, 98–102, 163–167
    see also hierarchical organiza-
        tion; management
business contacts, 157
business lunches, 150, 154–157,
    172–173

career development seminars, 72
    myth promoted by, 34–36
    reimbursement for, 158–159
    secretaries and, 83–84, 92–93
*Carroll v. Talman Federal Sav-*
    *ings and Loan Association of*
    *Chicago,* 58–63
chain-of-command, 13, 18–21
    see also hierarchical organiza-
        tion
Civil Rights Act, Title VII of,
    58–63, 161–162, 167–168
C.L.E.P. Tests (College Level
    Examination Programs), 132
clerical positions, secretarial jobs
    as, 84–85, 88–99, 100–101
Collins, Nancy W., 177
computer jobs, 71–74
conflicts, on-the-job:
    accommodation tactics for,
        65–67

201

recession (*cont.*)
  pressures on job hunting in,
    185–186, 196–197
  salary or wage restraints during,
    140–141
  sexism and, 50–52, 53–54
references, 180–185, 191–195
*Regulations, 541*, 82
relationships:
  with boss, 13, 18–21
  between bosses, 39
  business alliances, 14–16
  business vs. "humane," 8–9,
    40–43
  emotional responses in, 22–25,
    44–45
  management-staff kinship,
    23–24
  with past co-workers, 14–15
  romantic, 173–179, 188–191
relocation:
  advancement as dependent on,
    113–116
  as tool of exploitation, 115–116
  *see also* transfers
reorganization, authority shifted
  in, 31–33
resignations, 180–199
  disclosing reasons for, 180–185
  *see also* quitting
retail careers, 113–116
romance, 173–179
  effect of, on co-workers, 174
  in family firms, 188–191

salaries:
  as basis for promotion, 117,
    139–149
  for college professors, 112–123
  exempt/nonexempt regulations
    for, 78–83, 90
  headhunters and, 197
  industry influences on,
    146–150
  negotiating title vs., 107–110

  starting, 138–142, 145
  women's vs. men's, 19,
    135–136, 138–142, 148
  *see also* pay, pay scales
sales careers, 99–102
  expense accounts used in,
    150–152
  in industry, 167
secretarial careers, 83–102, 110
  changing attitudes in, 85–86
  job descriptions for, 84, 88–90,
    92–95, 97
  males in, 98–99
  as possible lifetime trap, 97–98
  raises negotiated in, 86–88,
    92–93
  shortage of, 87, 92
  as status symbols for manage-
    ment, 94–95
*Secretary, The*, 98
segregation, sexual, 135–136
sexism:
  accommodation tactics and,
    65–67
  anger as useful in dealing with,
    71–74
  daily employment logs in cases
    of, 76
  expanding definition of, 76–77
  recession and, 50–52, 53–54
  women isolated as aggressive
    in, 50–51, 71–77,
    163–167
  *see also* discrimination, gender;
    harassment, sexual
spouses, home entertaining and,
  170–173
  *see also* marriages
"staff" jobs, "line" jobs vs.,
  165–166
subordinates:
  alliances among, 14–16
  boss as protector of, 23–25,
    107–108
  further responsibility sought by,
    33–36

in hierarchy, 12–16
hostility of, toward boss,
    25–27, 99–102
overly ambitious, 34–36
*see also* hierarchical organization
summer employment, secretarial
    positions as, 96–98
supervisors, *see* bosses; hierarchical organization; management
support groups, 163–166

teamwork, 5, 7, 8–9, 12,
    125–126
T.E.F.R.A. (Tax Equity and Fiscal Responsibility Act of
    1982), 123
"temping," 195, 198
titles, 15
    "acting," 107–110
    authority vs., 13
    for secretaries, 83, 85, 92–95
training, on-the-job, 121–122
    postgraduate schooling vs., 121
    while schooling, 133
    special treatment during,
        28–31
    upward mobility as, 103–106
transfers:
    sexism escaped by, 74–76

*see also* relocation

uniforms, 54–63
unions, 147, 149, 166

*What Color Is Your Parachute?*
    (Bolles), 198
Wider Opportunities for Women
    (W.O.W.), 168
women:
    in beginning-level management
        positions, 28–31
    as bosses, 98–102, 163–167
    cultural conditioning of, 106,
        122
    insecure self-concepts of,
        52–53
    job approach common among,
        2–3, 26, 33–36, 72–73
    in nonprofit organizations,
        35–36
    overprotected, 24–25
    secretarial position as reflection
        of, 84–85, 87–99, 110
    without spouses, 170–173
    subservient stereotype of,
        52–54
    underpayment of, 19,
        135–136, 138–142, 148
Working Women's Institute,
    76–77, 169